The Collector's Encyclopedia of

OCCUPIED JAPAN

COLLECTIBLES

THIRD SERIES

Gene Florence

COLLECTOR BOOKS
A Division of Schroeder Publishing Co., Inc.

The current values in this book should be used only as a guide. They are not intended to set prices, which vary from one section of the country to another. Auction prices as well as dealer prices vary greatly and are affected by condition as well as demand. Neither the Author nor the Publisher assumes responsibility for any losses that might be incurred as a result of consulting this guide.

FOREWORD

Collecting items "Made in Occupied Japan" has grown into a very stable market in the last eight years since the release of my last book on the subject in 1978. There has been an increasing awareness among antique dealers who, heretofore, frowned upon anything not fifty years old. Now they have a shelf or two displaying their OJ wares. There is usually a sign accompanying the display espousing to all that pass—"Occupied Japan"!

For those readers who have not seen the previous editions, I will reiterate some basic information.

All items made in Japan (from the beginning of our occupation at the end of World War II until April 28, 1952, when the occupation ended), that were to be exported to the United States had to be marked in one of four ways: "Japan", "Made in Occupied Japan", "Occupied Japan" or "Made in Japan". You can see that if all the markings were used equally or nearly so, still only about half of the items imported into the United States would have been marked with the magic words for collectors, "Made in OCCUPIED JAPAN". Thus, too, you will find that there are many similar or like items which you will find marked only "Japan" or "Made in Japan". There is no way of proving these were actually made in "Occupied Japan". (For the sake of brevity, capital letters "MIOJ" and "OJ" will be used throughout the remainder of this book to mean "Made in Occupied Japan" or "Occupied Japan".) I must emphasize that unless an item actually says OCCUPIED in some form, it can not be considered to be such. The only exception to that rule would apply to items found in original containers such as boxes or cartons where the container is marked "MIOJ" while the items within are only marked "Japan". These items must always stay with the original container to be collected as OCCUPIED. From past observation and correspondence with collectors over the years, it is obvious that a large number of items imported from Japan during this time were marked on the containers only, and, of course, many of these original containers have been discarded. The original consumers did not care whether an item was marked "OJ" or not. These were governmental policies. It is speculated that only a small percentage of the larger, finer wares were themselves marked "MIOJ". The dearth of these marked pieces today makes them avidly sought by collectors and makes them very desirable to own.

It took eight years of buying to gather all the different, yet representative examples of "MIOJ" shown within these pages. All but three of the items in the book which were loaned were purchased by mother or me. We traveled from Washington to Hawaii to show you as many different items from as many areas as possible. From the 4000 or so pieces shown in my three books, I suspect that we are still only scratching the surface as to what is still available to be collected; and that's exciting!

I again urge you to be aware of quality items in your travels. If you have a choice between buying one quality piece or several smaller items, I recommend you consider buying the one. There will always be smaller items to be found, but the quality items are few and far between. If you pass up the opportunity to buy the item, you may never see it again except in a collector's displayed collection.

I have given as many measurements and markings as possible in this book. The measurements should help you in determining the value of a similar figurine. I get a lot of questions from non-collectors asking which color marking is the best to collect. Markings occur mostly in black or red, but there are many other colors found. I suspect that green was used less often than any other color, but I have never met a true collector yet who cared about the color of the marking.

There are a few fakes on the market that you need to beware of—from rubber-stamped marks to an importing company which has had a few bisque figurines manufactured from time to time. After a while you will be able to spot a piece of "OJ" from its "characteristic look". You will know it says "MIOJ" before you even pick it up to confirm it. Sure, you will pick up some that are only marked "Japan", as I do, but after a while it's a kind of sixth sense. The newly-made bisque figures have a different feel, color, and "look" to them. Find some bisque that you know is old and feel it. It is more porous and not very smooth. Now go to a gift shop and feel the bisque being made today. It is smoother to touch, not so rough. It will behoove you to learn these distinctions if you buy in places such as flea markets, garage sales or auctions. A dealer who sells "OJ" should know and stand behind his wares; as in most other areas, however, it is "Buyer Beware".

All the bisque fakes I have seen are marked "ANDREA" with an "ST". Anyone can make a mistake in buying once in a while; the best way to approach a mistake is to learn from it.

The rubber-stamped items I have seen employed block letters unlike any letters on pieces of "OJ" I had ever seen before. It is rare to pick up more than three pieces marked "MIOJ" in any one location without finding different markings on them. If you find a group of assorted objects at one time that all have the same marking, be wary. These could be stamped items.

If an object is glazed, the mark will be under the glaze. Nail polish remover or other similar substances will remove non-original marks. The only problem with this comes from the fact that not all items are glazed. Bisque never is glazed.

Some of you may wish to know there is now an Occupied Japan Collectors Club. The address is 18309 Faysmith Ave., Torrance, Ca 90504.

PRICING

All prices in this book are retail. The last thing I do for any book is to go over the prices, updating any new developments that may occur after the writing is finished. This is not as critical in "OJ" as in other fields of collecting, but with publishing lead times as they are today, I want you to know that the prices are current. I sell hundreds of pieces of "MIOJ" in my shop each year with one sale in excess of seven thousand dollars last year. I only mention this to let you know that the prices listed in this book are not "hoped-for" prices, but actual selling prices. Many of the items shown in this book will now be for sale in my shop; and by the time you read this, most of the best items will already have new homes. I try to spread the sale of the better pieces over a period of time, but if someone says, "I will take them all", then they own them!

You will see higher prices for "OJ" than are listed in this book; I am aware that you will find a few pieces cheaper than those listed here also. Yard and garage sales as well as auctions are good sources for finding bargains on "OJ", but more and more people are becoming aware of those magic words "MIOJ". Be prepared to pay a fair price and hope to find a bargain or two. You will see the same overpriced items time and time again in your travels. Remember that someday you may find the same item at an affordable price. If not, you can chuckle to yourself, as I do, over the prices as you see the item not selling again at shows or in a shop. Unfortunately, people with a little bit of knowledge about "MIOJ" sometimes think that they have a gold mine if they own it.

This book is meant as a guide only. The buyer and the seller determine actual worth. If a mutually agreeable price can be arranged between these two, then that is the price no matter what the book says! I buy and sell. I have to make those decisions often. Many times I leave pieces I would love to have but believe the price is out of line. You have to determine your limits as a collector. I repeat, these prices are meant to be a good, general guide.

Prices are listed as retail; thus, if you want to sell some of your collection to a dealer, you will have to discount them. Most dealers are willing to pay 50% to 60% of the retail price of most items. Common pieces or hard to sell items will be discounted more. Remember the better the piece or the more unusual it is, the more collectors will be looking for it.

Collectors are looking for mint items. The prices listed in this book are for mint condition items. That means having all the parts; no cracks, chips or glued pieces are acceptable. Unless it is very unusual and hard to get, there is very little value to damaged pieces.

One thing which is hard for some people to understand occurs in pricing dinnerware. The individual pieces of a set sell for more than the whole set. There are more people looking for pieces than there are for the whole set. In fact, it is harder to sell a set than it is to sell the cup and saucers. The cup and saucers determine the size of the set. You may have a service for twelve in all but the cup and saucers. If you only have eight of those, then you really have an eight piece set with extras.

As in the previous books, I have included a price range for each piece. Several collectors have told me, "I buy at low book and sell at high". Be your own judge. It is your money and only you determine how you spend it—unless you are married that is!

ACKNOWLEDGMENTS

There have been numerous collectors who wrote and shared their knowledge and collections with me. To them, I say thank you; and please know that I have treasured each morsel of information you have given me and that I have endeavored to share it with all my readers in this book.

My family has endured the time I have spent travelling and working on this book from buying and gathering, packing and photographing, and finally writing and typing. A special thanks to Cathy, note taker and proofreader. My sons, Chad and Marc, were glad to see the ping pong table free of "OJ" at last.

Figures and the records in the book were borrowed from Lisa Margarida, Pat Brumlon, and Peggy and Chuck Nixon. Gladys Florence loaned me many of her dolls and children's dishes. The rest of the items shown in this book are mine and will be for sale at my shop, Grannie Bear Antiques in Lexington, Kentucky. Drop in and see us if you are ever in the area.

The photography for this book was done by Curtis and Mays Studio in Paducah, Kentucky. The assembly line photography sessions, comments on the merits and demerits of the contents of this book and suggestions on how to dispose of many items herein were furnished by Jane Fryberger, Steve Quertermous, Bill Schroeder, Dana Curtis and Cathy Florence. Cathy messed up her back in the process and thus found a way to miss some of this "fun" we were all having. We all hope you enjoy the efforts and work we do for you, our readers.

TABLE OF CONTENTS

ANGELS and CUPIDS

As we begin our third journey in the collecting of "Occupied Japan", I would like to welcome you and hope you enjoy the voyage. A few words of explanation for those of you who omitted reading the beginning introductions. I will use the following references in this book: "OJ" means Ocupied Japan and "MIOJ" means Made in Occupied Japan. I will start by listing colors with the marks. If no color is listed, the mark will be in black unless otherwise noted. Most pieces are listed by size; I hope that will help.

High quality bisque figurines are most desirable to "OJ" collectors. You see examples of those on the first two rows of angels and cupids. Angels and cupids are always fun to collect because they are always poised to do something. More often than not, it is to play an instrument. My personal favorite here is the fifth cupid in Row 4. He seems to be repairing an arrow. Perhaps he shot it at a hard-hearted person and this was the result of that encounter.

Notice that there are several sets and partial sets shown. Garnering entire sets often interests collectors. The pair of vases shown on the ends of Row 4 are high quality workmanship and marked "Paulux". This mark occurs on some of the finest examples of "OJ" I have seen in my travels. You might wish to keep that in mind during your search.

Some collectors seek out the smaller pieces of "OJ" due to space limitations. So don't dismiss them as less worthy of consideration. They are often rather endearing as you can tell by the small angel bud vases in the last row.

Top Row:
1st and 3rd Flower Cupids, 4″ bisque	$ 25.00-30.00	ea.
2nd Cupid w/flower snail, 4½″ by 6″, bisque	30.00-35.00	

Second Row:
1st and 6th Cupid on sled, 5″ bisque, "MIOJ" (red)	30.00-35.00	ea.
2nd, 3rd, 4th and 5th Musicians, 3¼″ bisque, "MIOJ" paper label	7.50-9.00	ea.

Third Row:
1st Butterfly babe, 3¼″, "MIOJ" (red)	17.50-20.00	
2nd, 3rd, 4th and 5th Angels, 2″ to 2½″, "MIOJ" (red)	6.00-7.50	ea.
6th, 7th, 8th, and 9th Musician angels, 2½″	6.00-7.50	ea.

Fourth Row:
1st and 6th Angel vases, 7½″ bisque, "Paulux", "MIOJ" (red)	45.00-50.00	ea.
2nd Candleholder, 6″ bisque, "Andrea", "MIOJ" G450	40.00-45.00	
3rd Angel drummer, 5¼″ bisque, "Winter Hal-sey Fifth Ave., L&M "OJ"	25.00-30.00	
4th Angel w/horn, 5″ bisque, "OJ" (rust)	22.50-25.00	
5th Arrow repair cupid, 7″, "MIOJ" (red)	35.00-40.00	

Fifth Row:
1st Cupid w/donkey, 4″ bisque, "MIOJ" (red)	22.50-25.00	
2nd Nude on seahorse, 3½″, "MIOJ" (red)	17.50-20.00	
3rd Angel planter, 3½″, "MIOJ" (brown)	15.00-17.50	
4th and 5th Cupid w/moon, 3½″	8.00-10.00	ea.
6th and 7th Angel bud vase, 2¾″ "MIOJ" (black or red)	10.00-12.50	ea.

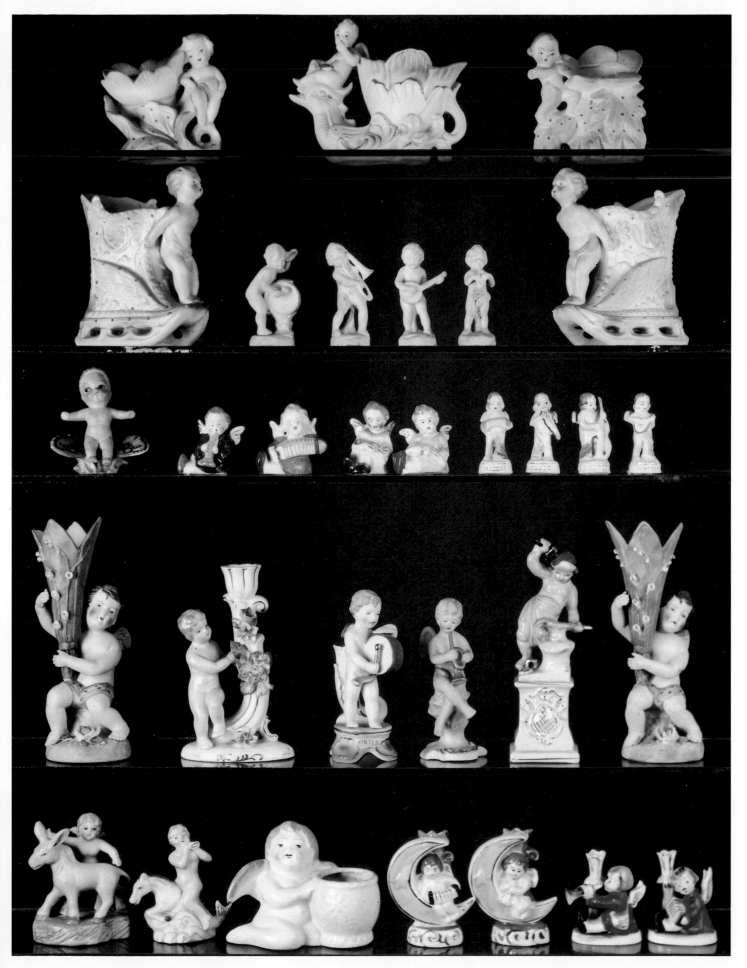

9

ANIMALS

Collecting animal figurines is by no means limited to those of us who collect "MIOJ". Collectors of scotty dogs, for example, are willing to pay higher prices for scotty dogs than many collectors who specialize in only "OJ". This not only presents a challenge to us, it also creates a healthy market for items that are sought in several collecting fields. Other overlapping collectibles on these pages are the pigs and flamingos. I can not believe the number of collectors now searching for those elusive "Miami Vice" pink critters.

On the opposite page is an assortment of four legged characters (including "Elsie" the cow!) with the dogs being the most collectible right now. In the bottom row are several partial sets. The lady bugs have their own band, but so do the monkeys. Maybe the cat and fiddle are watching for one of the cows in the top row to take a leap toward the moon.

Top Row:

Cow, 2¾″ x 4″	$ 8.00-10.00
Elsie, 3½″	17.50-20.00
Squirrels, 4½″ x 5″	17.50-20.00
Pig, 2½″ x 3½″	10.00-12.50
Cow set, large 2¾″ x 4″, small 1¼″	20.00-22.50

Second Row:

Horse, 2¼″	4.00-5.00
Cat, 2″	4.00-5.00
Cats, 1¼″	6.00-7.50
Dogs, 2¼″	8.00-10.00
Dogs, terriers, 3½″	12.50-15.00
Scotties, three white or black	6.00-8.00
Dogs in basket, 3¼″	10.00-12.50
Dog, blue, 1¾″ x 3¼″	6.00-7.50
Dog, 3¾″	10.00-12.50

Third Row:

Dog w/lamp, 2″	3.00-4.00
Dog, begging, 2½″	4.00-5.00
Dog w/pups, 2⅛″	4.00-5.00
Poodle, 3″	10.00-12.50
Shepherd, 1¾″ x 3¼″	5.00-6.00
Dog, green, 2″ x 3″	5.00-6.00
Dog pair, 2″	6.00-7.50
Dog w/horn, 3½″	7.00-8.50
Puppies, 2″, "Pico"	4.00-5.00

Fourth Row:

Dog, 4½″ x 5½″	12.50-15.00
Dog, 5½″ x 7″	12.50-15.00
Terrier pair, 4½″ x 7″	20.00-22.50
Terrier, 4″, "Ucagco"	15.00-17.50
Puppies in basket, 2½″	10.00-12.50

Fifth Row:

Lady bugs (3), 2¼″ x 2½″	6.00-7.50	ea.
Monkeys, white (3), 1¾″	4.00-5.00	ea.
Monkeys, (3), 2¼″	6.00-7.50	ea.
Monkeys, "Speak, see, and hear no evil"	10.00-12.50	
Cat w/fiddle, 2″	6.00-7.50	
Rabbit, 1″ x 2¼″	6.00-7.50	

ANIMALS—MOSTLY FEATHERED

The three ducks in the top row are the best examples of "OJ" wall plaques I have seen. They are exceptional in quality with beautiful feathers in vivid detail. Since my publisher is a duck hunter, they now decorate his office wall.

I mentioned the flamingos being highly sought, but I should point out that the covered hen on a nest in the fourth row is quite unusual. The penguin bookends in the bottom row are strange in that each is different. Normally, there would be the same number of birds on each piece or they would be mirrored opposites of each other.

Top Row:
Ducks, 5″ to 6½″, wall plaques, fine quality $ 20.00-22.50   ea.

Second Row:
Chicken pr., 5″	17.50-20.00
Bird, 3″	3.00-4.50
Ducks, 4″	10.00-12.50

Third Row:
Jay, 2½″	4.00-5.00
Crane, 3¼″	6.00-8.00
Peacock, 3⅛″	6.00-8.00
Bird, 2¼″	3.00-4.00
Bird, 2½″	4.00-5.00

Fourth Row:
Peacock, 7″	22.50-25.00
Chicken on nest, 5⅞″, 2 piece, "Mahumon Ware"	30.00-35.00
Flamingo, 5½″, Miami souvenir	12.50-15.00
Flamingo, 7¼″	20.00-25.00

Fifth Row:
Gazelles, 3¾″	7.00-8.50
Frog w/mandolin, 3½″, bisque	12.50-15.00
Frog w/violin, 4¼″, bisque	15.00-17.50
Frog w/accordion, 4″, bisque	15.00-17.50
Penguin bookends, pr., 4″	30.00-35.00

ASH TRAYS, LIGHTERS and MISCELLANEOUS

There are a few interesting cigarette lighters shown here that are collected by other than "OJ" collectors. In particular, the camera and guns are sought by collectors of those items as well as the Indian Chief's head sought by Indian object collectors.

In the fourth row are several good quality binoculars including one in its own case which is also marked "MIOJ". The first item in that row is a hand warmer which works!

Top Row:

Red bowl, 4¾"	$ 6.00-7.50
Horse pulling wagon, 3¼", spade on reverse, "Pico" ash tray	6.00-7.50
Tray, 8¾", alcohol proof	8.00-10.00
Horse pulling wagon, 3¼", diamond, "Pico" ash tray	6.00-7.50
Wash line ash tray	6.00-7.50
Tray, 9¼", "Highmount", alcohol proof	8.00-10.00
Lady ash tray, "Paulux"	12.50-15.00
Ceramic cigarette lighter, 2⅞"	15.00-20.00
North Carolina ash tray	12.50-15.00

Second Row:

"Wedgwood"-type, 2⅝" ash tray	8.00-10.00
"Wedgwood"-type, 4½", Niagara Falls Rainbow Bridge aero car	18.00-20.00
Metal lighter on tray, 5¼"	12.50-15.00
Donkey pulling ashes	6.00-7.50
Cigarette potties, souvenir of Concord, N.H.	12.50-15.00
Dog hydrant, 2 x 2¼", No Parking	4.00-5.00
Cigarette urn, 3", "Berkshire Fine China"	4.00-5.00
Lady spade ash tray	6.00-7.50
Metal four-piece set, 5¾", urn holder, lighter, tray and ash tray	22.50-25.00

Third Row:

Indian metal cigarette lighter	20.00-22.50
Urn type lighters, 2¾" and 3¼"	8.00-10.00 ea.
Round lighter, ball top, 4¼"	15.00-17.50
Giant lighter, 3" x 4"	15.00-17.50
Lighter set: lighter, 4 trays, cigarette box and stand, 3¼" x 6¼"	22.50-25.00
"Crown" lighter, 2½"	10.00-12.50
Gun lighter, 2"	15.00-17.50
Gun lighter, 2½"	20.00-22.50
Camera lighter	30.00-35.00

Fourth Row:

Hand warmer, 3¾" x 2½", blue velvet drawstring case, "Petersons"	25.00-30.00
Horse shoe ash tray w/horse, 4⅝", silver plate	20.00-25.00
Ash tray, 3½"	2.50-3.00
Binoculars, "Peafowl", 7 x 50, Field 710, No. 2611	50.00-65.00
Opera glasses	25.00-30.00
Ash tray, 3⅝", green and white	3.00-3.50
Binoculars w/case, "Prismex" coated lens, 8 x 30, Field 850, No. 2013	65.00-75.00
Horse ash tray, 4⅞"	6.00-7.50

Fifth Row:

Pink floral cigarette box w/four 3" trays, 3¾" x 2¾"	20.00-22.50
Floral cigarette box w/two 2½" x 3½" trays, 3½" x 4½"	18.00-20.00
Colonial ladies cigarette box with 2¾" x 3¾" tray, 3½" x 4½"	20.00-25.00
Violets cigarette box w/two 2¾" x 3¾" trays, 4" x 5", "Saji Fancy China"	22.50-25.00
Indian ash tray, 2¼" x 3¼"	6.00-7.50
Ash tray, 2¾" sq.	3.00-3.50

ASH TRAYS and METAL TRAYS

"MIOJ" metal items are some of the least sought collectibles in this vast range of items. There are a few avid collectors; but on a whole, this field of "OJ" collecting is widely ignored. Of major interest now are the "Statue of Liberty" pieces due to the renovation work being done and the "hype" accompanying it. Almost anything old which depicts "Her" is being collected. You will find that there are quite a few souvenirs of "Miss Liberty" marked "MIOJ".

Realize that a souvenir piece from your hometown is worth a small fortune if found near there; but the fortune diminishes greatly the further away you find it. Sioux Falls items will generally sell better in South Dakota than Kentucky.

VERTICALLY BY COLUMNS

Left Column Top

Ash tray, 3″, Basilique Ste. Anne de Beaupré	$ 4.00-5.00
Chicken clicker, 1½″	5.00-6.00
Elephant on world pencil trimmer	15.00-17.50
Ash tray, 3¼″, Montpelier, Vt.	4.00-5.00
Leaf, 5½″	4.00-5.00
Painted tray, 4″	4.00-5.00
Ash tray, 5¼″, Statue of Liberty	12.50-15.00
Nut bowl, 2¾″	4.00-5.00
Tray, 4¾″	3.50-5.00

Center Column Top

Ash tray, 4¾″, Indianapolis, Ind.	4.00-5.00
Bowl, 5″, Swan mark on back	6.00-7.50
Leaf, 6″	6.00-7.50
Leaf, 5″, "Economy"	4.00-5.00
Ash Tray, 4¾″, palm trees	4.00-5.00

Right Column Top

Ash Tray, 5½″	5.00-6.00
Divided trays, 5¼″ each representing the following:	
"Florida/Land of Sunshine" marked Sherry Fashions, Inc., Miami, Fla.	6.00-7.50
"U.S. Capitol/Washington Monument"	6.00-7.50
"Statue of Liberty/Empire State Building"	12.50-15.00
"Niagara Falls/Rainbow Bridge"	6.00-7.50
"World Famous Steel Pier/Auditorium & Convention Hall" Atlantic City, New Jersey	6.00-7.50
"Statue of Liberty/Crowd on beach at Moor Hotel," Coney Island	12.50-15.00

BISQUE GROUPS

These three groups represent some of the finest examples of "OJ" workmanship that I have seen in figurines. The planter at the top belongs to my Mom who collects rabbits. The detail is outstanding from the rabbit fur to the roses. She purchased this in Eastern Kentucky several years ago. It is marked "Paulux".

The middle item was found in Denver, Colorado, about five years ago. I was attending a Depression Glass show when a dealer approached me about the piece. She had it in her shop and said no one appreciated it because it was not German. She was tempted to scratch off the markings on the bottom and wondered if I would be interested in buying it. She told me the price to see if it discouraged me, and I told her to bring it in the next day. I thought it was exquisite and was surprised no one had been interested in it. My only problem was getting it back to Kentucky on the plane. I solved that by wrapping it in clothing and holding it in my lap all the way back. It has been in our china cabinet ever since with its first trip out being to this photography session.

The very large couple in the foreground is the heaviest and largest figurine group that I have ever seen marked "OJ". The only other marking is 'ST'. This piece came out of a very large collection I purchased in New Hampshire in the late 1970's. There are a few damaged flowers but this is a "find" in any sense of the word. Remember, the larger the size, the harder it is to find in "OJ". There are many collectors who are buying only larger pieces. All you need is money, patience and a lot of shelf space.

Top:
Planter couple w/rabbits, 5¼" x 7¼", "Paulux" $125.00-150.00

Right:
Cupid w/gold rings and lady w/lyre, 8¼" x 9¼",
   "Paulux"   200.00-225.00

Bottom:
Courting couple w/lambs, 8¼" x 9¼", "ST"   250.00-300.00

BISQUE PAIRS

Due to the difficulty of finding perfect pairs, there is a premium price being asked for pairs. I have indicated this below in my pricing. It is difficult enough to find large figurines, but in pairs, it is getting nearly impossible today. I must remind you I said PERFECT and not damaged or glued. I have turned down several figurines recently with glued heads, missing fingers and repainted surfaces. Know your dealer or examine every piece carefully.

Note the similarity in design for several of these. I have always been amused at the poses given to our rural people by the Japanese. It seems they do a lot of leaning on fences, picking flowers and playing instruments. We can not leave out all the dancers in our observations, but I have never been able to figure out their fascination with the Colonial style of dress. I suspect that close to fifty percent of all the figurines made in "OJ" are dressed in Colonial attire.

I might point out here that many bisque figurines have been damaged due to wrapping them in newspaper. The black ink rubs off and cannot be removed in many cases. Always wrap them in something clean and make sure this is done when you purchase them. It is maddening when you spend good money for perfect specimens and they are ruined when you get them home.

Top Row:

Orientals, 6", "MIOJ" (black)	$ 20.00 ea. or 45.00-50.00	pr.
Seated colonials, 7", "Andrea"	72.50 ea. or 150.00-175.00	pr.
Country couple, 6¼" male and 6" female	20.00 ea. or 45.00-50.00	pr.

Second Row:

1st and 6th pr. Vase, 5", "MIOJ" (red)	22.50 ea. or 50.00-55.00	pr.
Couple, 9¼", "Royal Sealy"	45.00 ea. or 100.00-110.00	pr.
Fence-leaning couple, 9"	57.50 ea. or 120.00-130.00	pr.

Third Row:

Flower gatherers, 10¼", "MIOJ" (black)	65.00 ea. or 140.00-150.00	pr.
Plumed hat couple, 9¾", "MIOJ" (red)	60.00 ea. or 125.00-140.00	pr.
Pastoral couple, 10¼", "MIOJ" (blue)	65.00 ea. or 140.00-150.00	pr.

BISQUE SINGLES

Most of the figures shown here are parts of sets. Since I could only find one, the title for these suited their condition. There are a few shown with little quality of workmanship or detail; but on a whole, these exemplify the finer "OJ" figurines to be collected.

Many of the higher quality bisque figures are comparable to the figurines of European countries. Without markings to indicate place of origin, many dealers would be hard pressed to believe the lady planter in Row 2 or the lady with the swan in Row 3 were not of German quality. The lady with the swan or cygnet is marked "Paulux" as is the third lady in Row 1.

Note that many of these figurines appear to be dancers or musicians so their partners are probably listeners or dancers also. Evidently the second lady in Row 2 has been used as a book end at one time. She has been weighted with sand or some other material and is quite heavy.

Top Row:

Colonial man, 7″	$ 25.00-27.50
Colonial man, 7″, "Maruyaima"	17.50-30.00
Lady w/basket, 7″, "Paulux"	30.00-35.00
Lady w/dog, 6″, "Hadson"	22.50-25.00
Man, 6½″	15.00-17.50
Windy lady, 6½″	25.00-27.50

Second Row:

Couple, 3½″ (red)	15.00-17.50
Lady w/basket, 6″ (red)	22.50-25.00
Lady shell planter, 5½″ x 6½″	45.00-50.00
Dancer, 5″	15.00-17.50

Third Row:

Lady, 4¾″ (red)	15.00-17.50
Lady, 4″	12.50-15.00
Horn player 4½″	15.00-17.50
Colonial man, 5″ (red)	12.50-15.00
Lady w/goose, 5⅝″, "Paulux" (red)	45.00-50.00

Fouth Row:

Lady w/fan, 10½″ (red)	65.00-75.00
Lady, 10¼″ (red)	60.00-65.00
Man w/flowers, 10¼″ (red)	60.00-65.00
Man w/violin, 9″	55.00-60.00

CELLULOID DOLLS

Collectors of dolls are more aware of these than many "OJ" collectors. The fact that these dolls are collected by more than one group of collectors means that they are in shorter supply than if they were sought by only "OJ" collectors. Many times I have seen these in doll dealers' booths labeled only as "celluloid" with no mention made of their being "OJ".

Finding these celluloid pieces with splits and cracks is no problem! The trick is to find mint condition pieces with a bonus being sometimes finding them in the original box. I have found a great demand for those in the crocheted dresses. Remember, these were bought to be played with; and if they were, survival for over thirty years is quite a tribute to their longevity. Celluloid was found to be extremely flammable. So, these aren't "good toys" for children.

Top Row:

Pink crocheted dress, 6″	$ 35.00-40.00
Nude, 4¾″	12.50-15.00
Pink baby, 5½″	20.00-22.50

Second Row:

Feather or go go dancer, 13″	40.00-45.00

Third Row:

Yellow and white crocheted dress, 8″	35.00-40.00
Kewpie, 2¾″	15.00-17.50
Feather dancer, 4¼″	12.50-15.00
Blue crochet boy, 7″	35.00-40.00

CELLULOID, DOLLS and TOYS

It is hard to miss the colorful water lilies which came out of old store stock in Hawaii. These were brought back by a soldier stationed on the Islands in the middle 1970's. He found these along with many other "MIOJ" items which were being sold by a lady who had closed her store in the early 1950's. It seems that Japanese products were not very popular in Hawaii. In fact, she went out of business and placed these items in storage. The stock from storage was being sold at a Drive-In Flea Market every Sunday morning.

The five dolls in the original box are supposedly the Dionnes, but how can one be sure without labeling to that effect. In any case, quints are not that common in any doll collection. Next to the quints are twins in a basket. Not only are the dolls marked, but the basket and the blanket are also. Black dolls were not common in this era; so they are highly prized by collectors of dolls, Black memorabilia, and Occupied Japan.

The plasterboard ducks with spring legs and elastic hangers are reputedly Donald Duck, but I can not confirm that. The magnifying glass has been well used, but it is the only one I have seen. Those shells fastened with "MIOJ" paper labels contain paper flowers.

Of all these interesting items, I found the paper squeeze accordian with the pictured swinging monkey the most fascinating. It still works!

Top Row:
Water lily in box $7.50-10.00 ea.

Second Row:
Dolls in basket, 4⅝″ x 3″, dresses and basket also
   marked   50.00-60.00
Quints in box, 2¾″, (Dionnes ?)   60.00-75.00

Third Row:
Dog, squeaker   8.00-10.00
Doll, china, 3¼″   22.50-25.00
Doll, china, 3″   15.00-17.50
Doll, black, 3¼″   35.00-40.00
Doll, 7″, dress marked also   40.00-50.00

Fouth Row:
Ducks, 4″ w/hangers and spring legs, paper labels   6.00-7.50
Magnifying glass   10.00-12.50

Fifth Row:
Shell w/paper flowers, 1¼″   2.50-3.00

Sixth Row:
Water lily   7.50-10.00
Celluloid dog house   8.00-10.00
Celluloid "Happy House" pencil holder   17.50-20.00
Paper monkey squeeze accordion, 1½″ x 2½″   10.00-12.50
Celluloid duck, 4½″   17.50-20.00

27

CHILDREN'S DISHES and TEA SETS

There have been many books written on this area of collecting. The most popular sets of our era are the "Blue Willow" and the Disney character sets. There was a "Donald Duck" set shown in my 2nd book; and I have seen "Mickey Mouse" sets also. Individual pieces and small sets are priced below as pictured on the right.

Set Prices "Blue Willow" or "Disney"

Two place setting consisting of: 2 cup & saucers, creamer, sugar w/lid, teapot w/lid (9 pieces)	$ 75.00-90.00
Four place setting consisting of: 4 cup & saucers, creamer, sugar w/lid, teapot w/lid, (13 pieces)	110.00-125.00
Six place setting consisting of: 6 cup & saucers, creamer, sugar w/lid 6 plates, teapot & lid (23 pieces)	200.00-225.00
Six place setting w/serving pieces: same as above but adds covered casserole and platter (26 pieces)	235.00-265.00

Set prices w/pieces as above in florals or other decorations.

Two place	20.00-22.50
Three place	22.50-27.50
Four place	35.00-40.00
Four place w/serving	50.00-60.00
Five place	40.00-45.00
Six place	50.00-60.00
Six piece w/serving	75.00-85.00

Top Row:
Blue Willow (Many styles and sizes)

Creamer, 1½" to 2"	8.00-10.00
Cup and saucer, 2¾" to 3½"	10.00-12.00
Plate, 3¾" to 4½"	12.00-15.00
Sugar w/lid, 2" to 2¼"	12.00-15.00
Teapot w/lid, 3¼" to 3¾"	30.00-35.00

Second Row:

Luster ware: 4 piece set consisting of: 2" creamer, 2" sugar, 3" teapot, 4) 2¾" cup and saucers	50.00-60.00
Luster creamer, 1½"	6.00-7.50
Blue Willow platter, 6"	15.00-17.50
Tomato teapot, 2" x 4"	12.50-15.00
Tomato cup and saucer	4.00-5.00
Tomato sugar w/lid, 1½" x 2"	7.50-10.00
Tomato creamer, (not shown)	5.00-7.50

Third Row:

Chest, 1½" high	6.00-7.50
Set: "Pico" w/2¾" tray, teapot, cr/sug. 2) cup and saucers	22.50-25.00
Bench, 1¾"	4.00-5.00
Refrigerator, 3½"	18.00-20.00
Set: 2¼" tray, w/cr/sug	10.00-12.50
Sink, 2" x 3"	18.00-20.00
Set: tray, teapot, pitcher, cup and saucer, cr/sug	20.00-22.50
Set: teapot, cr/sug, 4) cup and saucer	22.50-25.00
Refrigerator, Philco, 2½"	12.50-15.00
Cabinet, 2¼"	10.00-12.50
Dry sink, 2"	10.00-12.50
Sets: as shown marked HKATO	15.00-17.50

Fourth Row:

Chair, 3"	8.00-10.00
Chest, 1¾"	7.50-9.00
Couch, 3"	12.50-15.00
Chair, 3"	10.00-12.50
Dresser, 2⅛"	6.00-7.50
Chair, 1⅞"	5.00-6.00
Piano, 1¾"	6.00-7.50
Set: 1½" chest, 2¼" bed, 1¾" lamp table	15.00-17.50

Fifth Row:

Elephant w/flag, cup, 1¾"	8.00-10.00
Same, sugar w/lid, 2½"	10.00-12.50
Same, creamer, 1½"	8.00-10.00
Set: 1½" teapot, creamer (shown 3rd from end) sugar w/lid (not shown)	18.00-20.00
Set: teapot, creamer, 2) cup and saucers, sugar w/lid (not shown)	22.50-25.00

Sixth Row:

Set: sugar w/lid, creamer (not shown), 4) cup and saucers	45.00-50.00
Set: sugar w/lid, creamer, 4) cup and saucers, "Royal Sealy"	55.00-65.00

CHILDREN - "HUMMEL TYPE"

Figurines of children have been among the most popular types of "OJ" collectibles. Those which are similar in appearance to "Hummels" are being bought by other collectors than those who collect "OJ". Many of the "Hummel types" are direct copies of their German counterparts, but they do not have the quality of the originals.

The boy with broken sprinkler in Row 1 has an adorable expression on his face. I thought that it was damaged when I first saw it, but it is just made that way.

In Row 2 there is a begging dog and the last figure shows a very hungry duck which looks as if it might eat a small hand. The first and third boy and girl which are reading books are probably bookends in Row 3. There is enough detail to read her book which is a copy of "Little Red Riding Hood".

The middle gardeners in Row 4 are marked "Paulux". It seems he wants to dig up the sunflower while she is determined to water it. There is a forever tame bird sitting on the flower.

Top Row:
Boy w/broken sprinkler, 4½"	$ 30.00-35.00
Basket girl, 5½"	27.50-30.00
Basket boy, 5¾"	27.50-30.00
Flute-playing boy, 4½"	20.00-22.50

Second Row:
Skier, 4½"	25.00-27.50
Boy w/begging dog, 5"	35.00-40.00
Hiker, 4"	15.00-17.50
Girl w/basket, 4½"	15.00-17.50
Boy w/duck, 3¾"	27.50-30.00

Third Row:
1st and 3rd pr. (probably bookends), girl reading "Little Red Riding Hood", 5½"	35.00 ea. or 75.00-80.00 pr.
Umbrella pair, 6"	35.00-40.00

Fourth Row:
1st and 3rd Tyrolean pair, 5", different markings and colorations	35.00-40.00 ea.
Gardening pair, 5½", "Paulux"	45.00-50.00

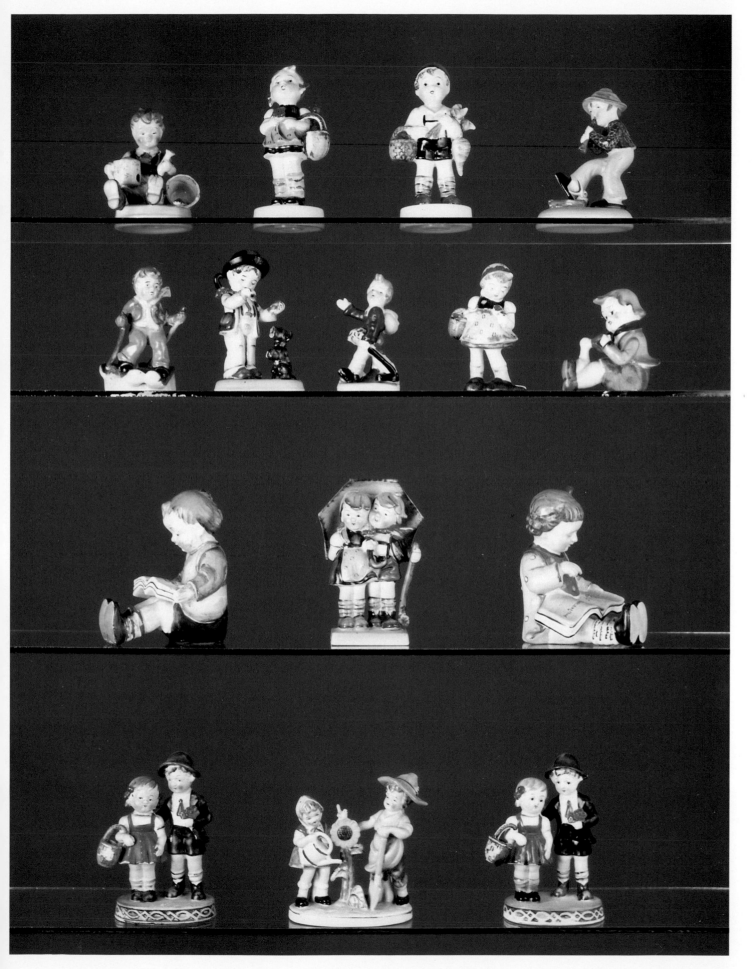

CHILDREN SINGLES

For some reason there is quite a group of musicians in this selection of children. The sizes are listed as is usual, but are deceiving because the girl horn player in Row 3 is so tall. She makes some of the other children seem smaller than they actually are.

The only child that seems out of place is the pugilist at the end of Row 1. Everyone else seems rather calm, but boxing gloves indicate insight into another side of American children of the 1950's.

The partial set of musicians in the bottom row have at least one more member and possibly two or three. I have only found the five for now.

All items are marked "MIOJ" unless noted otherwise. Color of mark in parenthesis.

Top Row:

Boy w/parrot, 5″ (red)	$ 10.00-12.50
Boy w/guitar, 4″ (turquoise)	7.50-9.00
Boy w/dog, 4¾″ (brown)	10.00-12.50
Girl, 4″ (black)	8.00-10.00
Boy w/horn, 3½″ (red)	6.00-8.00
Boy w/chick, 2½″ (black)	4.00-5.00
Girl on fence, 4″ (red)	8.00-10.00
Boxing boy, 4½″ (black)	10.00-12.50

Second Row:

Boy w/cello, 5″ (brown)	10.00-12.50
Accordian girl, 4½″ (red)	8.00-10.00
Horn player, 4″ (black)	10.00-12.50
Sax player, 4½″ (red)	8.00-10.00
Girl w/dog, 4¼″ (green)	8.00-10.00
Guitar player, 4½″ (red)	12.50-15.00
Book carrier, 4″ (black)	8.00-10.00

Third Row:

Boy w/hat, 5″ (red)	8.00-10.00
News boy, 5½″ (red)	10.00-12.50
Walker, 6″ (red)	18.00-20.00
Horn player, 9½″, "LD", (brown)	27.50-30.00
Tuba player, 5″ (red)	10.00-12.50
Musketeer, 5″ (red)	8.00-10.00
Hiker, 4″ (red)	10.00-12.50

Fourth Row:

Accordian player, 4″ (blue)	8.00-10.00
2nd to 6th Musicians, 2⅝″ (black)	6.00-7.50 ea.
Boy w/dog, 4⅛″ (red), store tag—Najarians	12.50-15.00
Violin player, 3¾″ (turquoise)	10.00-12.50
Flutist, 4½″ (red)	8.00-10.00

33

CUP and SAUCER SETS

The next eight pages show over a hundred cup and saucer sets with the last page showing purchases made in the last few months after our first photography session. This points out that there are still many of these available and you can collect all types from very plain to very colorful and from demitasse to regular dinnerware size. Later on, you will see a couple of sets large enough to hold your coffee for all day.

Remember that most of the interiors of the highly decorated sets are even more pleasing to the eye than the exteriors. Note how delicate many of the handles appear on the cups.

Many of these sets are from dinnerware or tea sets. In the 5th Row middle is a "Spring Violets" set representing a complete dinnerware set I recently encountered. I only mention that because not all the pieces in the dinnerware set were marked "OJ". What was unusual was that there were several odd items in the set such as butter pats and ash trays. I had never seen those pieces in any other "OJ" dinnerware patterns.

Top Row:
1st set "Merit"	$ 10.00-12.50
2nd set "Ucagco"	10.00-12.50
3rd set "Trimont China"	10.00-12.50
4th set "MIOJ" (red)	10.00-12.50

Second Row:
1st, 2nd, 3rd sets "Nasco Fine China"	8.00-10.00
4th set "MIOJ" (red)	10.00-12.50

Third Row:
1st and 5th sets "Shofu China"	12.50-15.00
2nd and 3rd sets "Ucagco"	12.50-15.00
4th set "Merit"	10.00-12.50

Fourth Row:
1st set "Merit"	12.50-15.00
2nd set "Gold China"	12.50-15.00
3rd set "Merit"	10.00-12.50
4th set "Noritake"	10.00-12.50
5th set "Jyoto China"	10.00-12.50

Fifth Row:
1st set "Jyoto China"	10.00-12.50
2nd set "Crown w/B inside" in red	12.50-15.00
3rd set "Spring Violets", Rossetti; Chicago U.S.A.	12.50-15.00
4th set "Elephant Head" w/A at end of trunk	12.50-15.00
5th set "Elephant Head" w/A at end of trunk	15.00-17.50

Sixth Row:
1st set "Lamore China" gold horse w/gray knight "exclusively GZI USA"	15.00-17.50
2nd set "Shofu China"	12.50-15.00
3rd set "Wako China"	15.00-17.50
4th set "Chugai China"	12.50-15.00

CUP and SAUCER SETS (Con't.)

Most of the descriptions below are adequate, but I would like to point out a few things. First of all, the very first set pictured was bought as a set, but it is not. Both are similar, but the quality of the cup is superb and the plate is not. You need to pay close attention that both the cup and saucer are marked the same in cases where there is doubt. These are not.

In the 4th and 5th Rows are some of the finer demitasse sets I have seen. I am particularly fond of the leaf-shaped cup set and those which have their own display stands. These stands are also marked "OJ" which is most unusual. It would have been nice to have found stands for all cup and saucers, but these are all I have seen.

Top Row:

Semi-nudes plate	$ 10.00-12.50
"Leawile China" (cup only) "Ardalt"	12.50-15.00
2nd set "Ironstone Ware"	12.50-15.00
3rd set "Trimont China"	12.50-15.00
4th set "Maruta China"	17.50-20.00

Second Row:

1st set "Ucagco China"	10.00-12.50
2nd set "Trimont China"	10.00-12.50
3rd set "MK" in wreath (orange)	10.00-12.50
4th set "MIOJ" (brown)	8.00-10.00

Third Row:

1st set "Merit"	8.00-10.00
2nd set "MIOJ" (red)	8.00-10.00
3rd set "Aiyo China"	12.50-15.00
4th set "Gold China"	10.00-12.50

Fourth Row:

1st set "Merit" (leaf shaped)	18.00-20.00
2nd set "Shofu China"	12.50-15.00
3rd set "Saji Fancy China"	12.50-15.00
4th set "MIOJ" (red)	8.00-10.00
5th and 6th "MIOJ" (red) stands for saucers also marked "MIOJ"	18.00-20.00 ea.

Fifth Row:

1st and 2nd sets "Saji Fancy China"	18.00-20.00
3rd set "Ohashi China"	15.00-17.50
4th set "MIOJ" (thatch house river scene)	15.00-17.50
5th set "MIOJ" (red pagota scene)	10.00-12.50

Sixth Row:

1st set "Trimont China"	12.50-15.00
2nd set "MIOJ" (green mark)	12.50-15.00
3rd set "Ucagco China" 'Ivory' pattern	12.50-15.00
4th set "Saji Fancy China"	10.00-12.50

CUP and SAUCER SETS (Con't.)

Some cups shown are missing saucers. However, I do not recommend buying separated cups and saucers.

For instance, I have been looking for a orange dragon saucer for over seven years and have found dragon sets in black, green and blue in the meantime. (They all came with saucers, thankfully). Unless you have unending patience, buy sets.

These cups and saucers are all marked in black unless noted in the listings below.

Top Row:

1st set "Merit"	$ 10.00-12.50
2nd set "MIOJ" (red)	10.00-12.50
3rd and 4th sets "Ucagco"	10.00-12.50
Blue flowered cup "Trimont China"	6.00-7.50
5th set "Gold Castle"	10.00-12.50

Second Row:

1st set "MIOJ" (red)	18.00-20.00
2nd set "MIOJ" (blue)	18.00-20.00
Orange dragon cup	12.50-15.00
3rd set "Lucky China"	15.00-17.50
4th set "MIOJ" (red)	18.00-20.00
5th set "Sak China"	12.50-15.00
6th set "Gold China"	10.00-12.50

Third Row:

1st set "MIOJ" (red)	8.00-10.00
2nd set "Merit"	8.00-10.00
3rd set "Saji Fancy China"	10.00-12.50
4th set "KS"	6.00-8.00
5th set "High Mount"	6.00-8.00
6th set "Ardalt" No. 6075	10.00-12.50

Fourth Row:

1st set "Ardalt" No. 6143	15.00-17.50
2nd set "Merit"	12.50-15.00
3rd set "Sango China"	12.50-15.00
4th set "Ucagco"	12.50-15.00
5th set "Celebrate"	10.00-12.50

Fifth Row:

1st set "MIOJ" (Designed by Aurger of Miami)	15.00-17.50
2nd set "Beteson China", J.B.	10.00-12.50
3rd set "Celebrate"	10.00-12.50
4th set "MIOJ" (brown)	6.00-8.00
5th set "MIOJ" (red)	8.00-10.00
6th set "MIOJ"	6.00-8.00

Sixth Row:

1st set "MIOJ" (red)	10.00-12.50
2nd set "MIOJ" (blue)	10.00-12.50
3rd set MB in wreath (blue)	10.00-12.50
4th set "Sanjo China"	12.50-15.00
5th set "MIOJ" (red leaf)	12.50-15.00

CUP and SAUCER SETS (Con't.)

The twenty sets pictured here were purchased after the first photography session and were taken to the studio when we reshot the late arrivals in the back of the book. It always amazes me the number of different cup and saucer sets that are available in "OJ". We bought fifteen sets from one lady and not one of them was shown in the earlier books or were in the prior photographs for this book!

There are several eye pleasers here as you can see. The snack set on the bottom row is probably part of a larger set, but there was only one available when I bought it in a shop specializing in old clothing. I find that vintage clothing shops often have other "vintage" items.

All sets are marked "MIOJ" in black unless noted.

Top Row:
1st set "OJ" (blue)	$ 10.00-12.50
2nd set "Ucagco China" (gold)	10.00-12.50
3rd set "OJ", "W" in wreath	15.00-17.50
4th set (red)	10.00-12.50

Second Row:
1st set "Ucagco China" (gold)	10.00-12.50
2nd set "Ucagco China" (gold)	10.00-12.50
3rd set (red)	10.00-12.50
4th set (red)	10.00-12.50

Third Row:
1st set (red)	10.00-12.50
2nd set (red)	10.00-12.50
3rd set (red)	10.00-12.50
4th set "Ucagco China" (gold)	10.00-12.50

Fourth Row:
1st set "OJ"	10.00-12.50
2nd set (orange)	10.00-12.50
3rd set "Trimont China"	15.00-17.50
4th set "Meito Norleans China", "Livonia"	10.00-12.50

Fifth Row:
1st set "Merit", "OJ"	12.50-15.00
2nd set (blue)	8.00-10.00
3rd set "Ucagco China" (gold)	15.00-17.50
4th set (orange)	10.00-12.50

DECORATIVE CHRISTMAS ITEMS

As I write this, it is approaching Christmas rather rapidly. Some of these are as appropriate to use today as they were some three decades ago. The decorations run the gamut of secular Santas to the religious symbols of the Nativity scene.

My particular favorite is the white clad skier in Row 2 which is similar to the highly collectible "snow babies" which were so popular at the turn of the 20th century. The detail on this skier is fine for its small size.

Most of the Christmas ornaments are cheaply made, but after examining what is available today, I doubt that the decorations currently sold will last as long. Notice the pipe cleaner Santas shown in Row 2!

The Santa planter in the Top Row is the type most collected by Santa collectors or so I have been told. Planters generally are made to be used for more than a short Christmas season. This makes the Santa planter a rare "OJ" item.

Top Row:

Celluloid reindeer, 7″ x 7½″ (sprayed silver)	$ 12.50-15.00
Santa planter, 5½″ x 6″	20.00-25.00
Tree, w/bulbs, 6¼″	7.50-10.00

Second Row:

Skier, 3½″, like snow baby	20.00-25.00
2nd, 3rd and 4th ornaments, 3½″, paper labels	6.00-7.50
Holly leaf package decorations, 4″ w/wire attachments	3.00-3.50 ea.
Santa pipe cleaner, 4″	10.00-12.50
Santa ornament, 4″	18.00-20.00

Third Row:

Nativity set, 7 piece, 2½″	35.00-40.00

Fourth and Fifth Rows:

Nativity set in paper mache' (figures from 2″ tall ox to 8¼″ angel but missing Christ Child)	125.00-150.00 set

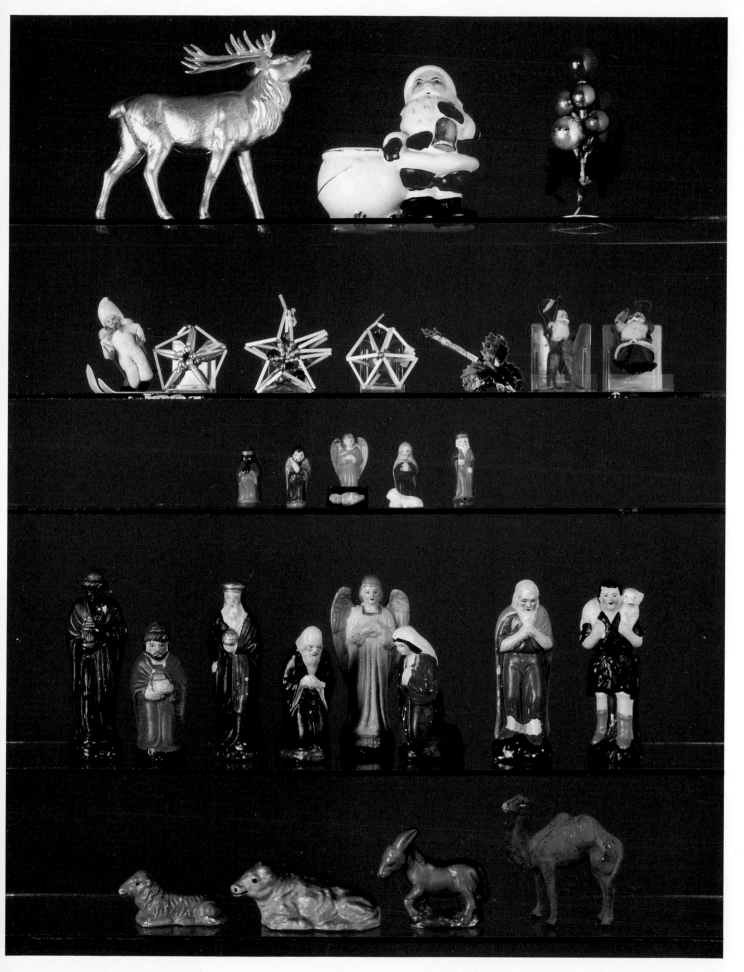

DECORATIVE CHRISTMAS ORNAMENTS

There are probably many of these "OJ" ornaments still in use today; however, the only marking for these is on the box. Unless the box has survived the many years of kids helping decorate the tree, there may be little left to announce that these ornaments were manufactured for us across the seas during the Occupation.

Of course, there are those of us who never throw anything away and others who bought extras after Christmas for half price and never got around to using them. To those savers and bargain hunters of yesterday we owe our heartfelt gratitude for keeping these available for collectors today.

VERTICALLY

Column One:

Box of 12 bells, "MIOJ" on box No. 51	$ 30.00-35.00
Box of 12 ornaments each 3¼" long	30.00-35.00

Column Two:

Box of 12 ornaments each 3¼" long, "MIOJ" on box No. 4	30.00-35.00
Box of 12 various designs each 2" long, "MIOJ" on box No. 207/6571 35m/m "Fancy Glass Ball Ornament"	17.50-20.00
"Christmas Tree Ornaments" 30m/m, 1 Doz., No. 32/822, "MIOJ"	12.50-15.00
"Glass Ball Ornament" 30m/m, 1 Doz. Maker "MIOJ", No. 207/2091	12.50-15.00

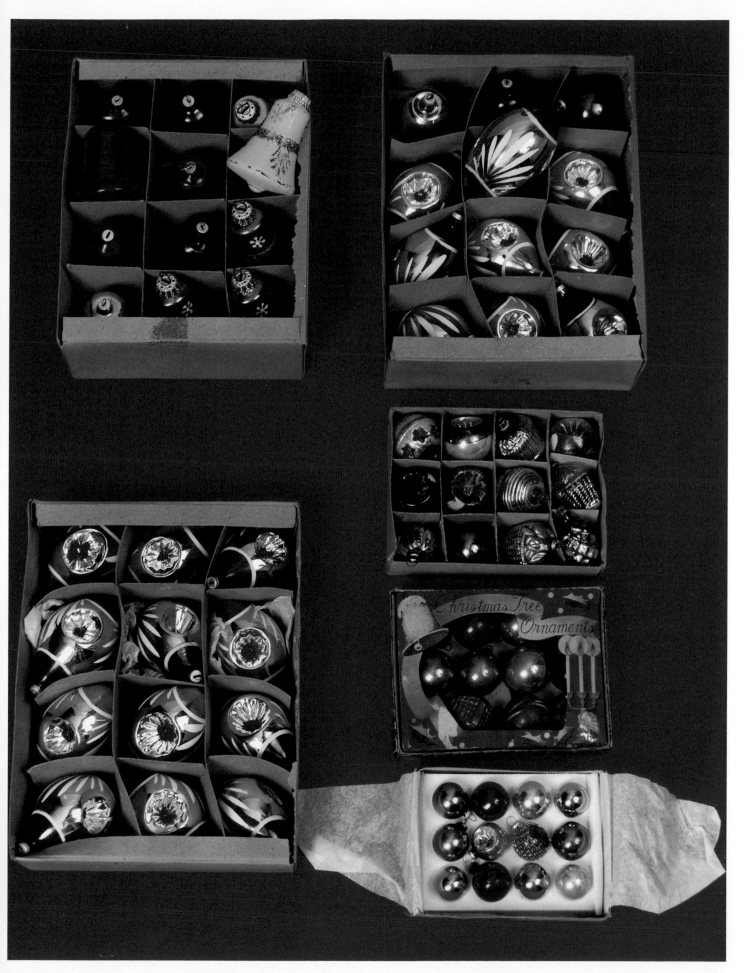

DECORATIVE ITEMS

Collectors of primitive ware are buying up all wall match safes. The brown one shown in Row 1 is only the second "MIOJ" I have been able to find. There are more of these available I am sure; but like many other "OJ" collectibles, there are collectors from other fields diminishing the availability.

The hanging planter in Row 3 with its own 24″ pottery chain I have seen marked both "MIOJ" and Japan. One of those without the "MIOJ" marking sold at a Mall antique show to an "Art Deco" collector for $90.00. It was exactly the same as this one except marked "Japan".

Those small handled plates in the bottom row make practical gifts for friends. Many times a small item such as this will start a new collector. Something old often makes a better gift than a brand "spanking new" item! This is particularly true of "OJ" items since their value keeps increasing.

Top Row:
Cup and saucer wall plaque, 3¼″	$ 6.00-7.50
Flower bowl, "Pico"	8.00-10.00
Snack plate, 9″ leaf, "Shofu China"	8.00-10.00
Match safe, 6¼″	30.00-35.00

Second Row:
Plate, 5″	6.00-7.50
Plate, 4½″, "Ardalt, 'Lenwile China' No. 3160"	6.00-7.50
Children's vases, 2″ pr.	15.00-20.00

Third Row:
Bowl, 7″	12.50-15.00
Plate, 6⅜″ "Shozan"	10.00-12.50
Hanging planter w/24″ pottery chain "Marumon"	50.00-65.00

Fourth Row:
Bowl, 5¾″ "Ucagco"	8.00-10.00
Handled leaf plate, 5½″	10.00-12.50
Handled plate, 5¾″	12.50-15.00

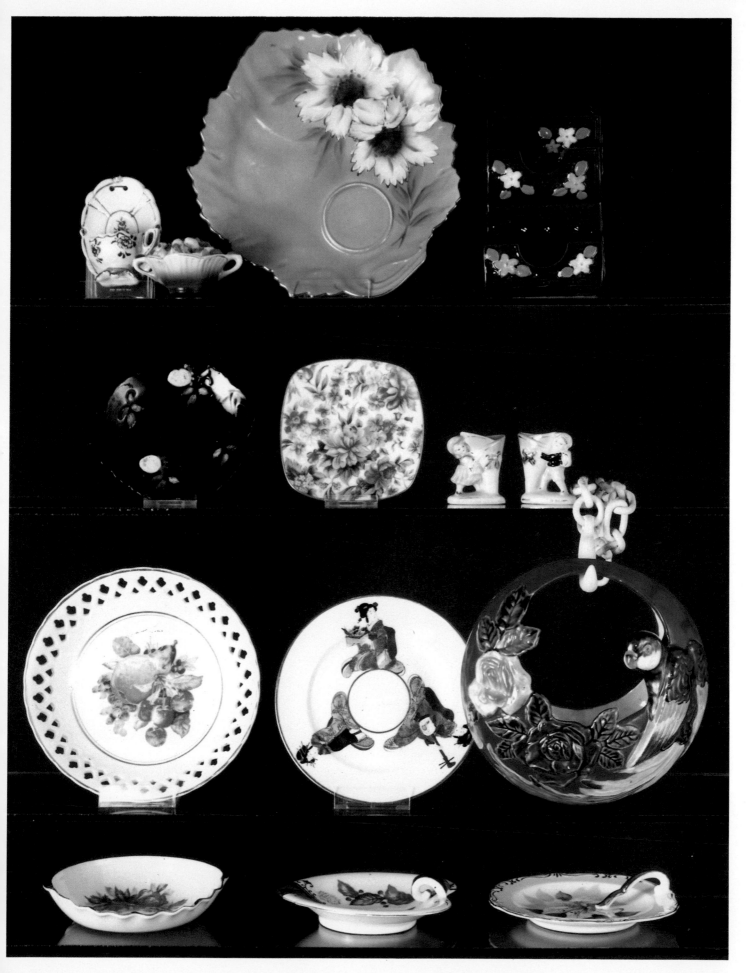

DECORATIVE ITEMS (Con't.)

Not knowing much about flowers, I was pleased that the makers of these plates listed the names of the floral designs on each of the plates shown in Row 1. What makes this interesting is that each of these were bought at different times in the last seven years and I was lucky enough not to duplicate any of the ones previously purchased. They are probably part of a set, but I have no idea how many plates, or varieties of flowers, make up the set.

The china plates shown in Row 3 are reminiscent of European styles of years ago. The open lace effect is superb and would be passed off as fine quality early china if it were not marked "OJ". Often this open laced plate is termed a "ribbon plate" due to their being sold with ribbons wound through the lacings.

Top Row:
Plates, 8¼", "Rosetti" Chicago, USA $ 20.00-22.50   ea.
"Cup of Gold"
"Hibiscus"
"Hybrid Cattelya"

Second Row:
Handled divided tray, 10", Elephant head mark   10.00-12.50
2nd and 3rd plates, 3¼", souvenir Carter Caves, Olive
   Hill, Ky.   5.00-6.00   ea.
4th plate, 3⅜", Lake Champlain   5.00-6.00
Flower frog w/seven holes, unusual, 4½"   10.00-12.50

Third Row:
Bowl, 6"   10.00-12.50
Plate, 7¾", "Ardalt, 'Lenwile China' No. 6327"   20.00-25.00
Plate, 8", exceptional quality   65.00-75.00
Bowl, 6"   10.00-12.50

Fourth Row:
Leaf, 6½", "Ucagco China"   8.00-10.00
Leaf, 3", "Kyokuto China"   4.00-5.00
Leaf, 5½", "Chubu China"   10.00-12.50

Fifth Row:
Plates, 6⅛", "SGK China", "Andrea"   20.00-25.00   ea.

DINNERWARE

There has been a new trend in collecting sets of dinnerware that are "MIOJ". Many collectors are collecting smaller sets or a sample setting. This type of collecting plus others who are trying to fill in old sets has lessened the demand for full sets. What has occurred now is that the price of a set is cheaper than all the pieces if sold seperately. This is true in many other areas of collecting such as coins or baseball cards. It takes a long time for a dealer to sell out each and every piece of a set. He would rather sell the whole set at a cheaper price than take years to sell each piece one by one.

Because of that, I am now pricing sets as a whole and the individual items. Smaller sets are in demand due to the high costs of large sets. Many times it takes years to find a collector for a particular pattern, but if you have the pattern someone is looking for, you will have a friend for life.

I will only list those pieces which I have. There are additional pieces; so be aware of that.

Pattern: "Livonia" (Dogwood by collectors) by Meito Norleans China

Bowl, 5¾", cereal	$ 6.00-7.50
Bowl, 8⅞", soup	7.50-9.00
Bowl, 7¾" x 12" w/handles, casserole	35.00-40.00
Creamer	12.50-15.00
Cup	10.00-12.50
Gravy boat	15.00-17.50
Gravy platter, 9¼"	10.00-12.50
Plate, 6½", bread and butter	3.50-4.00
Plate, 7⅝", salad	5.00-6.50
Plate, 10½", dinner	12.50-15.00
Platter, 13½"	15.00-17.50
Platter, 18¼"	25.00-30.00
Saucer, 6½"	2.00-2.50
Sugar w/cover	17.50-20.00

Set for 4 including: cups, saucers, plates in 3 sizes, cereal and soup bowls, creamer and covered sugar	175.00-200.00
Set for 6 including all of the above for 6 and gravy boat and platter	225.00-250.00
Set for 8 including all of above for 8 and small platter	275.00-300.00
Set for 12 including all above for 12 and adding casserole and large platter	400.00-450.00

DINNERWARE (Con't.)

Be sure to read previous page about collecting dinnerware.

The set shown here has no name on the back. Most patterns do. It was "MIOJ" by Yamaka China and that is all I know except that it is a beautiful floral pattern. The name was probably on the box!

There are additional pieces to this set; so be aware that you may find others not listed here. Let me know what you find.

Bowl, 5½", cereal	$ 6.00-7.50
Bowl, 7½", soup	8.00-10.00
Bowl, 7½" x 11", oval	15.00-17.50
Creamer	10.00-12.50
Cup	10.00-12.50
Gravy boat	15.00-17.50
Gravy platter, 9¼"	10.00-12.50
Plate, 6⅝", bread and butter	3.00-4.50
Plate, 7⅝", salad	5.00-6.50
Plate, 10¾", dinner	12.50-15.00
Platter, 12¼"	17.50-20.00
Saucer	2.00-2.50
Sugar w/cover	15.00-17.50
Set for 4 including: cups, saucers, plates in 3 sizes, cereal and soup bowls, creamer and covered sugar	175.00-200.00
Set for 6 including all of above for 6 and gravy boat and platter	225.00-250.00
Set for 8 including all of above for 8 and small platter	275.00-300.00

DINNERWARE (Con't.)

The name Noritake is the most widely known company in Japan today. At least as far as making china goes, it is. Their china was widely distributed at the better department stores of the Occupation era. One of the problems for "MIOJ" collectors is that they were so successful that many of their sets of china were still carried for years after the Occupation ended. What that means is that many replacement pieces bought later were not marked "OJ" and many "Noritake China" sets are mixtures of both "OJ" and "Japan". You will get arguments both ways as to whether or not this is acceptable to collectors. Collectors I know have balked at buying pieces that match but are not marked "OJ". Suit your own desires and realize the prices here are for "MIOJ" only.

There is no name to the pattern shown here. It is marked "Noritake China" with M in a wreath over a bow. Prices shown here are for this pattern. A more colorful "Noritake" set could bring 10 to 15% more.

Not all pieces to this set are shown. You will find others.

Bowl, 5¾", cereal	$ 6.00-7.50
Bowl, 8⅛", soup	8.00-10.00
Bowl, 10", round vegetable	15.00-17.50
Bowl, 10¾", oval vegetable	17.50-20.00
Creamer	10.00-12.50
Cup	10.00-12.50
Gravy boat w/attached platter	22.50-25.00
Plate, 6⅜", bread and butter	3.50-4.00
Plate, 7¾", salad	6.00-7.50
Plate, 10", dinner	12.00-13.50
Platter, 14¼"	20.00-22.50
Saucer	2.00-2.50
Sugar w/cover (cover not shown)	12.50-15.00
Set for 4 including: cups, saucers, plates in 3 sizes, cereal and soup bowls, creamer and covered sugar	200.00-225.00
Set for 6 including all of above for 6 and gravy and platter attached	250.00-275.00
Set for 8 including all of above for 8 with platter and vegetable bowls	325.00-350.00
Set for 12 including all of above for 12 with additional serving pieces	450.00-500.00

DINNERWARE - MISCELLANEOUS, ETC.

Top Row:

Plate, 10″, "Empire Shape, Meito China, Ivory China"	$ 8.00-10.00
Demitasse cup and saucer, "Highmount"	6.00-8.00
Plate, 7½″, "Hira China"	6.00-8.00
Plate, 10″, "Empire Shape, Meito China, Dexter, Ivory China"	7.00-9.00
Cup, "Merit China"	6.00-7.50

Second Row:

Demitasse cup and saucer, souvenir sticker	6.00-8.00
"Blue Willow" cup and saucer	12.00-15.00
"Blue Willow" bowl, 5″, "Kakusa China"	6.00-7.50
"Blue Willow" egg cup, 3¾″	15.00-17.50

Third Row:

Plate, 5⅝″, marked K in circle	8.00-10.00
Demitasse cup and saucer, "Ucagco China"	8.00-10.00
Plate, 7½″ (same as 1st)	10.00-12.50
Sugar, (same as 1st)	12.50 w/o lid, 15.00-17.50 w/lid

Fourth Row:

Platter, 10″ x 14″, "Ironstone Ware"	25.00-27.50
"Blue Willow" child's tureen, 5″ x 2¾″	20.00-22.50

ETHNIC FIGURINES

Japanese depiction of other cultures seems to rely heavily on stereotypes. Highly collectible are the Black and American Indian figures whether "OJ" or not.

Row 3 depicts what I have been told are Buddha gods. These are made of a very different type of material than most figures. It seems to be the same substance that sometimes is left unglazed. It is a very soft, porous substance that I am unfamiliar with in other ware.

I might make note of the little red man in the bottom row. He may be the Martian representative as conceived by the Japanese artists of the 1950's. Other than that, I have no idea as to what he represents. The Indian in the canoe is shown later as a set of salt and peppers. Some ingenuous person evidently made a floral decoration after breaking one of the shakers. Shows you what a little imagination will do to preserve what has now become a collectible.

All figures are marked in black unless noted.

Top Row:

Black fiddler, 5″	$ 30.00-32.50	
Black fiddler, 6″	40.00-45.00	
Indian squaw, 4½″ (red)	10.00-12.50	
Indian (Asian), 6″ (red)	12.50-15.00	
Balloon lady, 5½″	40.00-45.00	
Indian w/papoose, 5½″ (red)	20.00-22.50	
Indian planter, 3″	8.00-10.00	
Indian Chief, 5½″ (red)	20.00-22.50	
Indian squaw, 6″ (red)	25.00-30.00	

Second Row:

Black band members, 2¾″	18.00-20.00	ea.
Chinese couple, 5¼″ (red)	20.00-22.50	
Buddha, 5½″, embossed mark	20.00-22.50	
Incense burner, 4″ (red)	20.00-22.50	
Dancer, 5″ (green)	22.50-25.00	
Black shoe shine boy, 5½″ (red)	45.00-50.00	

Third Row:

Religious symbols, 4″ to 4¾″	6.50 ea. or 47.50-50.00	set

Fourth Row:

Dutch water girl, 4″	10.00-12.50	
Dutch planter, 3″, "Pico"	12.50-15.00	
3rd and 5th Delft ladies, 6¼″ (blue)	32.50-35.00	ea.
Dutch girl w/milk can, 6″ (red)	20.00-22.50	
Dutch children, 3″	10.00-12.50	ea.
Dutch egg timer w/sand timer missing in picture, 3½″ complete	20.00-22.50	

Fifth Row:

Eskimoes, 3″ and 2¾″	12.50-15.00	ea.
Indian water boy, 4″ (red)	10.00-12.00	
Indian, 3″ (red)	8.00-10.00	
Spanish guitar player, 4¼″ (red)	8.00-10.00	
Mexican, 5¼″	17.50-20.00	
Martian (?), 3″	20.00-25.00	
Indian canoe w/plastic flowers	18.00-20.00	

FIGURINE GROUPS

As pointed out in my previous editions, statues with more than one person depicted are hard to find. I suspect that these were harder to make.

There are several size coaches as shown in Row 2. This is what I would call a medium size being 7″ long. The larger ones are about 10″ in length.

My favorite of these is the last pair shown in the bottom row. It seems that a scene has been stolen from an early movie with the villian making his move on the sweet young heroine. Maybe this gal is destined for the railroad tracks if she spurns his attention.

All figurines are marked "MIOJ" in red unless noted.

Top Row:

Couple at piano, 4″	$ 20.00-22.50	
Dancing couple, 4½″ (black)	18.00-20.00	
Triple, 3″	12.50-15.00	
Romantic couple, 4″	20.00-22.50	
Couple, 4½″, "Canadian National Exhibition, Toronto, Canada"	17.50-20.00	
Couple, 4″	12.50-15.00	

Second Row:

1st and 4th Serenading couple, 5¼″ and 5⅛″	18.00-20.00	ea.
Coach et. al., 5¾″ x 7″	50.00-55.00	
Serenading couple, 4½″ (black)	15.00-17.50	
Triple w/piano, 3¾″	22.50-25.00	

Third Row:

Couple waiting for rain, 5½″ "Highmount" (green)	22.50-25.00	
2nd and 3rd Couples, 5½″ and 5¼″	18.00-20.00	ea.
4th, 5th and 6th Couples, 4¼″ to 3¾″	12.50-15.00	ea.
Couple, 4½″	15.00-17.50	

Fourth Row:

1st, 3rd and 4th Couples, 6⅞″ to 6⅜″, 3rd marked "ST"	30.00-35.00	ea.
Musicians, 7″ x 7⅞″	45.00-50.00	
Villain and captive, 7½″ (blue)	40.00-45.00	

FIGURINES · ORIENTAL PAIRS

You can see the detail in most of these figurines. Even the smaller ones seem to exhibit some personal traits. Note that there are many dancers and musicians. One difference I see between the Oriental pairs and our American Colonials is that the Western ladies were shown with many flowers and the Eastern ladies are shown with fans.

In Row 2, the first four figures are all marked the same. I have not been able to decide if they are part of a larger set, if this is the set, or if these are two pairs that are similar in make-up. Maybe, it shows two generations, or perhaps I am reading too much into it!

The couple with outstretched hands in Row 2 might be the bases for salt and pepper shakers. Sometimes tomatoes or other objects which held these condiments were hung on outstretched hands of figurines like these.

All items are marked "MIOJ" in black or red unless noted.

Top Row:

Dancers, 5″	$ 15.00 ea. or 35.00-37.50	pr.
Robed in red, 6⅛″	20.00 ea. or 42.50-45.00	pr.
Pair, 5⅞″ and 6″	20.00 ea. or 42.50-45.00	pr.
Pair, 6½″ and 6″	22.50 ea. or 47.50-50.00	pr.

Second Row:

1st and 2nd pairs are all marked the same, 4½″	12.50 ea. or 27.50-30.00	pr.
"It was this long", 4¼″	15.00 ea. or 32.50-35.00	pr.
Musicians, 4½″	15.00 ea. or 32.50-35.00	pr.

Third Row:

Dancers, 7½″	22.50 ea. or 47.50-50.00	pr.
Dancers, 8⅛″	30.00 ea. or 62.50-65.00	pr.
Couple, 7¾″ and 8″	30.00 ea. or 62.50-65.00	pr.

Fourth Row:

Couple, 7½″ and 7⅜″, "Mariyama"	27.50 ea. or 60.00-62.50	pr.
Dancers, 8¾″	42.50 ea. or 90.00-100.00	pr.
Prayerful couple, 7⅝″, "Mariyama	25.00 ea. or 52.50-55.00	pr.

FIGURINES — ORIENTAL SINGLES

All of these shown are singles except for possibly the 5th and 6th figures in Row 4. They are marked the same and have the same shaped bases. The only concern that I have about these being paired is that he is seated and she is standing. Normally, both figures of a pair are in a similar pose.

I have noticed a trend over the last few years that has indicated that the "OJ" collectors in my area are buying Oriental figurines faster than any other kind. When I have bought small collections for the shop, it was the Orientals that were sold out first. I can not say for sure that this is a trend nationally, but it is true for my area.

Large and good quality figurines are foremost finds - for any "OJ" collectors. There are many fine quality Oriental figurines available, but to find any that are eight or more inches tall takes some serious searching. The 10″ musician is the tallest Oriental I have ever seen. He is of only average quality unfortunately; but I would like to see the lady who goes with him.

Top Row:

Grandfather, 6″	$ 25.00-27.50
Warrior, 8″	35.00-40.00
Girl w/bird, 6″ (blue R in shield)	22.50-25.00
Girl, 7⅛″	25.00-27.50
5th and 7th, Coolie and musician, 7″ and 6½″	22.50-25.00 ea.
Holding flowers, 6″	20.00-22.50

Second Row:

Lady w/flowers, 5½″	18.00-20.00
Bended knee flower offering, 5″, "Maruyema"	18.00-20.00
3rd and 5th Musician and lady, 5″	15.00-17.50 ea.
Girl w/bow, 4½″	12.50-15.00

Third Row:

Instrument player, 9″	44.00-45.00
Lady w/muff, 8″	30.00-32.50
Musician, 10″	60.00-65.00
Warrior, 8¼″	35.00-37.50
Robed man, 8″	32.50-35.00
Woman, 7½″	25.00-27.50

Fourth Row:

Lady w/fan, 5″	15.00-17.50
Baldy, 4″	15.00-17.50
Coolie, 3¼″	10.00-12.50
Coolie, 4″	12.50-15.00
Man w/rabbits, 4″, "Ardalt, Lenwile China"	35.00-40.00
Lady w/fan, 3¾″, marked as above	32.50-35.00
Dancer, 4½″	18.00-20.00

FIGURINE PAIRS

Most of these pairs are good quality. Those on the top row are more difficult to find. As pointed out previously, groups of more than one person are very elusive. The second courting couple is marked "Mariyama" and has excellent detail and workmanship. Notice the faithful dog at the girl's side. Pairs with animals are considered choice items to own.

In Row 2 the busts are unusual and there are collectors of these besides "OJ" people. At the end of that row is a seated couple, extremely detailed; marked "Paulux".

In Row 4, the shepherd and shepherdess are two of the largest figurines I have found in almost twenty years of looking at "OJ". The 7″ pair next to them is dwarfed by comparison; and that 7″ pair would be a great find on any day!

All items are marked "MIOJ" in black or red unless noted.

Top Row:
Double pair, 6″ $ 30.00 ea. or 62.50-65.00   pr.
Courting couple double, 6″, "Mariyama"   55.00 ea. or 115.00-125.00   pr.

2nd Row:
Busts, 5½″   17.50 ea. or 37.50-40.00   pr.
Trio, 4″ and 3¾″   12.50-15.00   ea.
Seated couple, 5½″, "Paulux"   40.00 ea. or 85.00-90.00

Third Row:
Double, 4¾″   12.50 ea. or 27.50-30.00   pr.
Musician and friend, 5″   15.00 ea. or 32.50-35.00   pr.
Couple, 5″   10.00 ea. or 22.50-25.00   pr.

Fourth Row:
Flower holders, 7″   30.00 ea. or 65.00-75.00   pr.
Shepherds, 13½″   75.00 ea. or 160.00-175.00   pr.
Dancers, 6¼″ and 6″   20.00 ea. or 42.50-45.00   pr.
White dancers, 6¼″   15.00 ea. or 32.50-35.00   pr.

FIGURINES - SINGLE LADIES

Most figurines are found in pairs or sets, but I was unable to find the mates to these; so, they have been dubbed as "single ladies".

Notice again that the ladies are mostly shown three ways: playing instruments, dancing or gathering flowers—all very feminine, lady-like pursuits. Rosey the Riviter evidently wasn't deemed "sellable".

The most significant figurines to many collectors are the large ones in the bottom row. Both of these are over 10" and there are very few "MIOJ" figures that stand that tall. Size and quality are the two most significant factors to consider in buying figurines. There are other considerations, but those are the most important for the investment purposes. Prices for larger pieces are presently not much more than you will pay for new figurines bought from the gift shops of today. In many cases the smaller ones can be purchased for less than new ones.

All are marked "MIOJ" in red or black unless noted.

Top Row:

1st, 2nd and 3rd Ladies, 4"	$ 10.00-12.00	ea.
4th, 5th and 6th Dancers, 3¾" and 4"	12.50-15.00	ea.
Ballerina, 4½", net dress	22.50-25.00	
Ballerina, 5¾", net dress	35.00-40.00	

Second Row:

1st, 3rd and 4th Figures, 5¼" and 5"	18.00-20.00	ea.
2nd Cellist, 3¼"	12.50-15.00	
5th and 7th Figurines, 4¼"	12.50-15.00	ea.
6th Figure, 4"	10.00-12.00	

Third Row:

Lady, 5"	18.00-20.00	
2nd, 6th and 8th Ladies, 4¾" and 5"	12.50-15.00	ea.
3rd and 5th Flower ladies, 5" and 5⅜"	15.00-17.50	ea.
4th and 7th Ladies, 4 and 4¼"	10.00-12.50	ea.

Fourth Row:

1st and 11th Figurines, 7" and 6¼"	22.50-25.00	ea.
2nd, 4th and 8th Flower ladies, 4¼" and 4"	10.00-12.50	ea.
3rd Mandolin player, 10¼"	45.00-50.00	
5th Lady, 12¼"	65.00-75.00	
6th Windy flower girl, 5"	15.00-17.50	
7th and 9th Ladies, 7" and 6¾"	27.50-30.00	ea.
10th Peddler, 3½"	8.00-10.00	

FIGURINES - SINGLE MALES

As stated before, I call these singles since they were found that way. They most likely are one of a pair or set. Notice that the predominant dress is Colonial style for the men. There seem to be many dancers and flower toters, but only a few musicians.

In order to match up pairs or sets you need to look at the following: pedestal type, size, decoration, and marking. The size of pairs always seems to fall within ¼″ of each other with the male being taller if there is a difference. You will see by measurements of pairs later that they are almost always the same height. The bases of pairs will always have the same shape and usually they will be colored or decorated the same. The "MIOJ" or "OJ" marking will be the same color, style and design.

You might, for example, find a lady to match one of the two Colonial men in the bottom row. The one way to be sure which one is her mate (if you can not tell from decoration) is to look at the mark. One of these is "Orion China" and the other is "Paulux". Of course, you might find one you will think matches and it is neither. That is what makes this interesting, the search for pieces to match those you already have. Of course, that can also be frustrating when it turns out that you find what you think is a match and it is not.

All figurines are marked "MIOJ" in red or black unless noted.

Top Row:
Man w/hat, 7¼″, "Morirama"	$ 27.50-30.00	
2nd and 3rd Men, 8″	35.00-40.00	ea.
Man, 7½″	27.50-30.00	
Seated, 6¼″	22.50-25.00	

Second Row:
Man w/flowers, 5″	15.00-17.50	
2nd, 5th and 6th men, 4″	12.50-15.00	ea.
3rd Man, 3″, "Pico"	8.00-10.00	
4th Man, 3½″	8.00-10.00	
7th Waver, 5½″	18.00-20.00	

Third Row:
1st and 2nd Men, 6″ and 6½″	27.50-30.00	ea.
Bottle boy, 5¼″	18.00-20.00	
4th and 5th Men, 6½″ and 6″	20.00-22.50	ea.
Violinist, 5⅜″	12.50-15.00	

Fourth Row:
1st and 5th Men, 8″ and 7½″	35.00-37.50	ea.
Uniformed man, 10⅜″	60.00-65.00	
Colonial, 10″, "Orion China"	65.00-75.00	
Red head, 9¾″, Paulux	65.00-75.00	

GLASS OBJECTS

I was amazed to get a letter a few years ago from a Michigan reader who wanted to sell me some stemware that had paper labels ("OJ") on it. Never having seen or heard of "OJ" stemware, I acquiesced. It is not high quality glassware and, in fact, looks like plastic at first glance. There were four sizes and several duplicates. The label says "Pioneer, Superior Glass Ware, OJ".

Any glass objects "MIOJ" are rare; but there are a couple that I need to talk about here. It is hard to see, but Row 2, 3rd item is very unusual. I have seen these single wedge-shaped perfume bottles before and wondered why that shape. The three bottles, pink, green and blue form a circle and sit on a round glass tray. I thought I would never top those until the stemware turned up.

Row 4 shows a Parrot lamp which still works (with batteries). It is a little temperamental at the switch; but the original bulb still works. I have also seen this lamp with an owl in place of the parrot. They do not give off much light, but that would be desirable as a night light.

All objects are embossed "MIOJ" on the glass unless noted.

Top Row:
1st to 4th Stemware, 4¼" to 5¼", paper label, "Pioneer,
    Superior Glass Ware" $ 15.00-17.50   ea.

Second Row:
Pink atomizer   20.00-22.50
Blue atomizer   25.00-27.50
Perfume set, pink, blue, and green wedge shaped bottles w/stoppers on round tray   45.00-50.00   set
Blue cologne and atomizer on blue tray (each piece
    marked)   50.00-55.00   set

Third Row:
Blue atomizer   25.00-27.50
Animals w/paper stickers   6.00-7.50   ea.

Fourth Row:
Parrot lamp, metal embossed "MIOJ", "Reliance,
    Chicago" souvenir of Compton, Ca. (works
    w/batteries)   75.00-85.00
Crystal perfume and stopper   20.00-22.50
Green pair of atomizers   27.50 ea. or 57.50-60.00   pr.

Fifth Row:
Perfume, pink or green   15.00-17.50   ea.
Blue perfume   17.50-20.00
Perfume, green or pink   17.50-20.00
Pink perfume   20.00-22.50
Blue perfume w/unusual stopper   22.50-25.00

JEWELRY · BOXES · PURSES

In Row 1 is a wooden cigarette box showing three of the popular brands of that day. The second box in that row has sliding doors which open to reveal a hand-painted scene.

The crocheted purse in Row 2, as well as the drawstring basket-type, are both unusual and the only larger type purses I have seen in "OJ". There are quite a few of the wooden boxes with secret compartment openings. The hidden notched opener is exposed so you can see it. Evidently the butterfly brooches were a dime store item. You press the wings together to open the feet which clamp to your clothing.

The large jewelry box plays "Für Elise" for the dancing geisha girl. This was an expensive box when new and is quite ornate in decoration.

Top Row:

Wood cigarette box, 3½" x 5", sections for "Lucky Strike", "Camel" and "Chesterfield"	$ 35.00-40.00
Wooden jewelry box, 7½" x 7¾"	65.00-75.00
Bead string, 60" long, paper label	25.00-30.00
Chest, 2 drawer, 3" x 4½"	20.00-22.50

Second Row:

Crochet purse, 5" x 8½", cloth sewn-in label	60.00-75.00
Wooden box, secret compartment, 4" x 7"	30.00-35.00
Butterfly brooches, spring clip-on	4.50-5.00 ea.
Bead purse, drawstring top, basket bottom, 7" x 7½", cloth label	60.00-75.00

Third Row:

Geisha dancer music box, 12" x 5" closed, blue and white paper label	150.00-175.00
Rosary beads, 30", metal cross stamped "MIOJ"	30.00-35.00
Pearls, 16", paper label	
Harmonica bracelet, 7½", "Pee Wee"	20.00-22.50
Pearl bracelet, paper label	18.00-20.00
Gold expansion bracelet, band embossed "MIOJ"	20.00-22.50
Purple beads, 24", paper label	18.00-20.00

LACQUERWARE, WOOD ETC.

The lacquerware corner shelves fold up flat. They are folded and hooked together with the shelves resting against a notch. Being neat and easy to store makes them useful today also, and a great place to display some of your "OJ"!

There is a multitude of the alcohol-proof coaster sets available on today's "OJ" market in all sorts of decorations as evidenced by a couple on Row 2. The wooden set in Row 3 is a different matter. There are few of these found as is the case with most wooden "OJ" except for salad bowls. Someone must have convinced the American public that a wooden bowl was the only thing from which you could eat salad. In any case, the distributor for wooden salad sets did a fantastic job of promotion as shown by the number in existence today.

Primitive collectors are latching onto all the salt boxes available which leaves few for "OJ" people. The clothes hanger is something I did not notice the first time I saw it, but after buying a collection with one in it I have now seen a few more. That is what is fascinating about "MIOJ"; there is no telling what you may find!

Top Row:
Net dress and hat lady, 6″	$40.00-50.00	
Corner shelf, 9¼″	40.00-45.00	
Chest, 3″ x 4¼″, three drawer	35.00-40.00	

Second Row:
Coaster, 4¼″, "Highmount Alcohol Proof"	3.50-4.00	ea.
Box, 5″ x 2″ which holds 8 coasters of above	27.50-30.00	set
Dancer, 4¼″, "Paulux"	25.00-30.00	
Box set of coasters, 7 only marked "ISCO" in diamond	27.50-30.00	set
Coaster, 4¼″ for set	3.50-4.00	ea.

Third Row:
Relish, 3 part, 5¾″ x 15″, made by "Bafuri Hand Patented Lacquerware"	50.00-55.00	
Wooden coaster box and six 2¾″ coasters	25.00-30.00	set

Fourth Row:
Salt box, 5″ x 5″, "Ucagco" mark	45.00-50.00	
Corner shelf, 13¾″, two shelf	65.00-75.00	
Dancer, 4″, net skirt	20.00-25.00	
Wooden clothes hanger, 10″ x 10″	22.50-25.00	
Wood salad bowl, 10″	15.00-17.50	
Wood salad bowl, 6″	6.00-7.50	ea.

LAMPS

Can you spot the pair that is really not a pair? In Row 2 the first "pair" is really not a pair. To be a true pair the man will be on the outside on both lamps or as a mirror image of the other. This occurs in all couple groups be it lamps or plain figurines. Since these are the same it is not a true pair as it was intended. Above and below these are true pairs of lamps.

All lamps shown here are porcelain except for the first pair in the bottom row which is bisque. Most of these are in Colonial dress and a majority of all the lamps that were "OJ" seem to be in that period of dress. The lamp that is most unusual is the lady's head in Row 1. I assume that there is a man's head out there which matches her in some description or manner. Let me know what you find!

The lamps with metal bases have to be taken apart to find the "OJ" marks on the porcelain bottoms. All of these lamps are wired and ready to use; but we hid the cords behind the lamps for photography purposes.

All lamps are measured to socket top.

Top Row:
1st and 2nd Double pair, 11″	$ 30.00 ea. or 65.00-70.00	pr.
3rd Couple, 10½″, metal base comes off to reveal mark	30.00-32.50	
4th Couple, 10½″, "Chikuoa" (green)	32.50-35.00	
5th Male bouquet holder, 10″	27.50-30.00	
6th Lady's head, 10″	40.00-50.00	

Second Row:
1st and 2nd Double pair, 10½″	30.00 ea. or 65.00-70.00	pr.
3rd Musician and singer, 11½″	30.00-32.50	
4th Dancing couple, 11½″, "Pioneer MDSE Co., N.Y. 1950"	45.00-50.00	
5th Courting couple, 10″	32.50-35.00	

Third Row:
1st and 2nd Colonial bisque pair, 11″	50.00 ea. or 105.00-115.00	pr.
2nd, 3rd and 4th Couples, 10″ and 11½″	35.00-40.00	ea.

LINENS

It has always amazed me that when you find one of *something you have never seen before,* that before you can turn around, there are more to be found. I hadn't located any linen items for the first two books. I went to a Depression Glass show in Lima, Ohio, and brought one linen set there. Within six months I had found four other sets of napkins with a tablecloth! If these had ever been used, the fact that they are "OJ" would have been lost due to the fact that they all have paper labels except for the plaids in Row 4. The plaids have sewn-in tags.

Most of these were given as wedding gifts and never used according to the sources from which I purchased them. The peach colored set in the bottom row was still in its original wrapping tissue and had never been untied. It was left that way for over thirty years, so I did not want to change its status just to photograph it.

Top Row:
"Fleur de lis" design consisting of four 10″ square
    napkins and one 32″ square tablecloth. These have
    paper labels. $ 75.00-85.00   set

Second Row:
Damask set consisting of four 12″ square napkins and
    one 48″ x 52″ tablecloth. These have paper labels.   85.00-100.00   set

Third Row:
Linen set consisting of four 10½″ napkins and one 32″
    square tablecloth with paper labels attached.   80.00-90.00   set

Fourth Row:
Tablecloth, red plaid w/yellow and blue, 48″ square,
    sewn-in tag   40.00-50.00
Tablecloth, red and white plaid check, "Hadson Cloth,
    cotton/rayon, No. 211, 50″ x 50″, "MIOJ"   35.00-45.00
Set of four damask napkins, 12½″ square, flower
    decorated w/green/pink/blue blossoms   12.00 ea. or 50.00-52.50   set

Fifth Row:
Embroidered blue/ecru towels, 13″ x 17″   20.00-22.50   ea.
Peach tablecloth and napkin set, paper label (never
    opened)   75.00-85.00   set
Napkins, 12½″ square, gray w/paper labels   10.00-12.00   ea.

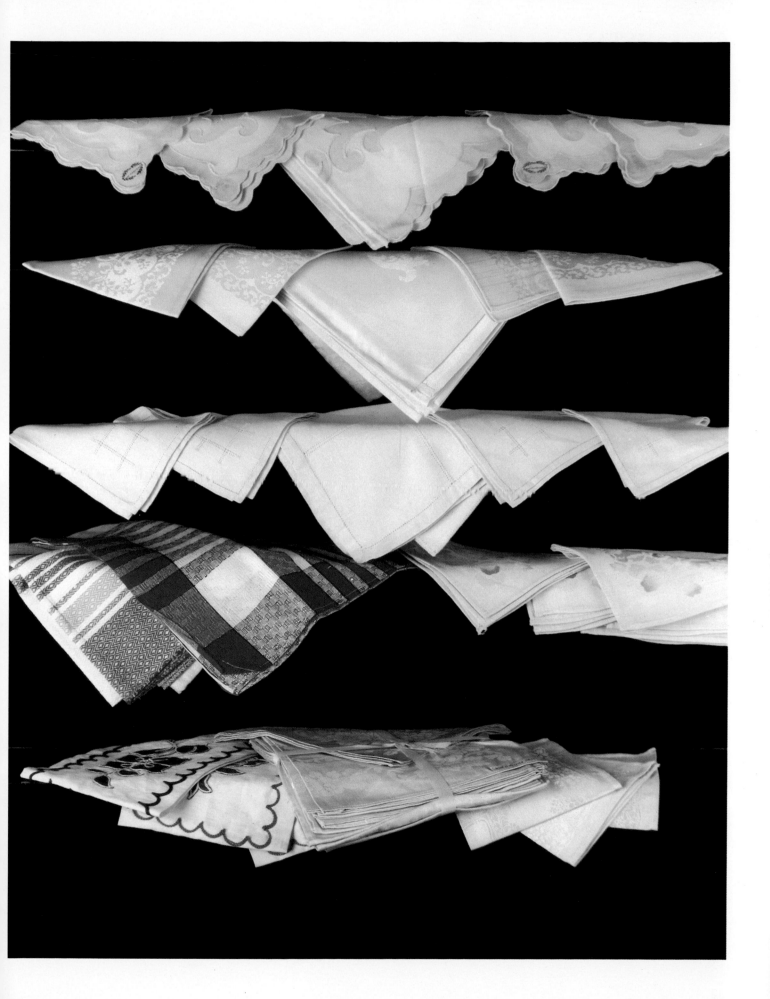

METAL

Metallic objects are probably the least collected of all "OJ" objects. The renewed interest in the Statue of Liberty renovation has caused some demand for souvenir items associated with it. There are many of these shown in the following pages and they are selling faster than any other souvenirs except for local items of interest. An item in your local area will bring more than it will any place else.

The third column down beginning with the wind-up turtle contains the most interesting items shown here. The turtle crawls very slowly, but most of them do! The puzzles are described below, but they are much more difficult to solve than they look. Putting that mouse in the trap while putting the eyes in the cat gave us a few minutes of diversion at the photography session. Everybody had to try their hand at it!

VERTICALLY BY COLUMN
Column 1 Top:
Butler, 5¼″ x 6″ $ 8.00-10.00
Copper butler, "Capital Souvenir, Inc.", A CAPSO
    Prod. Shows five Washington, D.C. scenes   8.00-10.00
Butler, N.Y. souvenir showing four scenes including
    Statue of Liberty   12.00-15.00
Crumb butler   6.00-7.50
Crumb butler, souvenir of Washington, D.C.   5.00-6.50

Column 2 Top:
Tray, 9½″ x 4½″   7.50-9.00
Tray, 4¾″ x 2″, souvenir of United Nations   8.00-10.00
Golden tray, 4¼″ x 5¾″, marked "MIOJ" w/eagle   6.00-7.50
Ash tray, 4¾″, souvenir of N.Y.C. w/Statue of Liberty   12.50-15.00

Column 3:
Turtle wind-up toy   20.00-25.00
Puzzles w/mirror on back, 2¼″   8.00-10.00 ea.
    Clown (put eyes and eye lashes on face)
    Dog (put eyes and eye lashes on face)
    Cat (put eyes in cat and mouse in trap)

Column 4 Top:
Ash tray, N.Y.C. souvenir w/Statue of Liberty   10.00-12.50
Heart trays souvenirs of Montreal, Canada and New
    Orleans   6.00-7.50 ea.
Trays, 5″ x 3½″, souvenirs of New Mexico and
    Washington D.C.   5.00-6.50 ea.

METAL (Con't.)

The items pictured here and on the next page represent some of the better quality metal objects I have found. Since there are few collectors for metallic objects, a dealer has to learn to stock those items which are in demand. In demand means ones that are unusual, unique or of quality material or workmanship.

Some items to note are the tall candlesticks in the top row (short ones are found fairly frequently) and the Buddhas shown in Row 4. There are only six shown here and they are numbered on the bottom from 1 to 6. I assume that there may be another one as there are seven shown in another category in the book.

Top Row:

Covered sugar, 2¼" x 5"	$ 10.00-12.50	
Creamer to match	5.00-7.50	
Candlesticks, 5" pair	22.50-25.00	
Jewel box, 2" to 3½"	8.00-10.00	
Jewel box, 2½" x 3½"	10.00-12.50	

Second Row:

Scotty dog covered box, 2½" x 3½"	12.50-15.00	
Miniature teapot, creamer, covered sugar on tray, 4"	22.50-25.00	
Covered butter, 3¼" x 4½"	15.00-17.50	
Salt and pepper shakers, 1⅜"	10.00-12.50	
Jewel box, 3" x 3½"	12.50-15.00	
Creamer and sugar on 7¾" tray, embossed TFK, "MIOJ"	22.50-25.00	set

Third Row:

Salt and pepper shakers, 2¼"	15.00-17.50	
Cigarette urns, 3"	7.50-8.50	ea.
Covered sugar	12.50-15.00	
Jewel box, deer on top	12.50-15.00	
Jewel box, Pegasus type horse on top	15.00-17.50	
Tea strainer	10.00-12.50	

Fourth Row:

Buddha gods, 2⅛", (each numbered 1-6 and shown 4,6,2,3,5,1)	8.00-10.00	ea.
Crown box, 3" x 3½", silver plate	15.00-17.50	
Niagara Falls souvenir piano box	15.00-17.50	
"Pico" piano box	15.00-17.50	
Salt and pepper, 3" souvenir of Niagara Falls	15.00-17.50	

Fifth Row:

Souvenir ash trays of various descriptions	3.00-3.50	ea.
Special trays such as Statue of Liberty	8.00-10.00	ea.

METAL (Con't.)

There are some quality metal pieces which are sought by collectors and some are shown here. In Row 3 are a well designed and detailed horse and sulky, handled candlesticks and a silverplated salt and pepper on tray. I have seen many "OJ" pieces that looked silverplated, but this is the only one I have seen marked as such.

The bottom row contains two very nice jewel boxes. The first is dragon covered and the other is designed so that it takes a key to open its lock. Most box lids just lift to open; but this is different. By the way, the keyhole was inadvertently turned to the back when photographed in case you are looking for it.

Top Row:

Jewel box, 3½″ x 4½″	$ 12.50-15.00	
2nd and 4th Vase, 8″, 15.00 ea.	32.50-35.00	pr.
3rd Vase, 7″	15.00-17.50	
Cigarette box, 3½″ x 4¼″	18.00-20.00	

Second Row:

1st and 3rd Sugar and creamer on 7½″ tray, embossed swan mark	22.50-25.00	ea.
2nd Miniature set in 4″ tray (missing lids)	15.00-17.50	

Third Row:

Horse and sulky, embossed camel mark	22.50-25.00
Salt and pepper on tray, 5⅜″, silverplated, embossed world w/wings mark	25.00-27.50
Handled candlestick, pair	22.50-25.00

Fourth Row:

1st and 2nd Piano jewel boxes, 2½″ x 3″, world w/wings mark	12.50-15.00	ea.
Bowl, 6¼″	8.00-10.00	
Piano box, 2¼″ x 3½″	12.50-15.00	

Fifth Row:

Dragon covered box, 4″ x 7″, crown mark	22.50-25.00
Salt and pepper on tray, swan mark	17.50-20.00
Jewel box w/lock, 3¾″ x 6¾″	22.50-25.00

MISCELLANEOUS - Bank, Bells, Bookends, Candle Holders, Ring Boxes, etc.

The range of items here defied description. Most were porcelain but even that was too general so I took the catch-all way out with "miscellaneous". Bookends, bells and candlesticks, that reminds me of an old movie starring Kim Novak.

The bookends in the top row do not match and I suspect that there are matching male counterparts. You will note that the pair in Row 4 contains a male and female.

In Row 3 are two bells, a chef and Mrs. ? I have not seen any other "OJ" bells. The elephant in that row is the only porcelain bank I have seen. Last year someone sent a photo of a cast iron bank which I found hard to believe was "OJ". I never did hear any evidence to collaborate whether it was or not.

Powder boxes are eagerly sought by collectors and there are a couple of beauties here. See Row 4, the 3rd lady and the 3rd lady in the Row 5. The latter is bisque, and seated on a swing. The top looks like a wall plaque but lifts off to reveal a bottom storage area.

All items are marked "MIOJ" in black or red unless noted.

Top Row:

Bookends, 4½" x 5½", non-matching	$ 17.50 ea. or 35.00-40.00 pr.
Candleholders, 4"	22.50 ea. or 50.00-55.00 pr.
Elf on snail, 4¼" (blue)	27.50-30.00

Second Row:

Purple elf, reclining	12.50-15.00
Green elf, sitting	15.00-17.50
Colonial lady double candleholder, 4"	20.00-22.50
Colonial lady single candleholder, 4"	17.50-20.00

Third Row:

Accordian playing elf, 3¼"	15.00-17.50
Lady bell, 3"	22.50-25.00
Chef bell, 3"	22.50-25.00
Mushroom elves, 1⅝"	10.00-12.50
Elephant bank, 2¼" x 3¾"	25.00-30.00

Fourth Row:

Clown, 4"	10.00-12.50
Clown, 4½" marked "EL" in circle	17.50-20.00
Powder jar lady, 5¾"	30.00-35.00
Clown, 6¼"	22.50-25.00
Bookend pair, 4 x 5½"	17.50 ea. or 37.50-40.00 pr.

Fifth Row:

Blue powder jar, 2½"	8.00-10.00
Heart w/windmill scene, powder jar, 2¾"	10.00-12.50
Bisque lady in swing powder jar, 7½"	45.00-50.00
Heart w/"Plymouth Rock, Mass.", 2¼" (blue)	8.00-10.00
Blue w/rose powder, 3½"	12.50-15.00
"Wedgwood" type box, 3¼" x 2"	15.00-17.50

MISCELLANEOUS - Sewing Items

This photo contains some odd items to say the least. A customer of mine brought in the silk scarf. Note the sewn-in tag hanging below it. The inscription is written below in the price list.

In the top row is a baby sweater that an about-to-be grandmother found when going through her daughter's baby clothes that she had kept. It is well preserved and 100% wool.

The lamp scarves in Row 3 are ones I purchased right before photographing the second book. The book was photographed in our living room right after we moved into this house in 1978. In all that ordeal I did not find these until after the book was already on the market. I have not seen any others since that time.

The picture on the bottom row has to be rated as highly unusual. In talking to collectors of many years, no one has seen anything like it. It is done in embroidery. It had a cellophane cover which we removed to eliminate glare in the photo.

Top Row:
Silk scarf, "Hand Pure Rolled Silk, 'Top Hit' Fashion,
    BARR & BEARD, INC.", 48″ x 18½″, "MIOJ" $ 45.00-50.00
Baby sweater, "100% Wool, Dist. by Carolyn Mfg. Co.,
    Haddad & Sons Props., New York, MIOJ"   40.00-45.00
Cat pin cushion, 3½″ x 5¼″   15.00-17.50

Second Row:
Right side Organdy crewel scarf, 11″ x 5¼″   18.00-20.00

Third Row:
Lamp scarves, 10¾″ square, paper label   25.00-27.50 ea.

Fourth Row:
Celluloid tape measure, 3″ girl   15.00-17.50
Heart box   4.00-5.00
Sewing kit, mirror in lid, 6 spools of thread, thimble,
    embossed "MIOJ" on paper cardboard bottom   18.00-20.00
Picture, "Omi Art Embroidery Co., ECHIGWAICHO,
    SI-UGA-KEN, JAPAN, Best Embroidery, Sataro
    Tritoni"   45.00-50.00

NOVELTY ITEMS

To be perfectly honest, I avoid buying these novelty items unless they are of good quality, unusual, or catch my eye. Most of what is shown here comes from buying collections. Everything that was brought into the shop for purchase was checked to see if it was pictured in the earlier books. If not in those books, it was packed away and only unpacked this summer when I started to get this book together. Some of the 2000 plus pieces in this book have been packed since 1978. It would stagger your imagination to know how few items were duplicated in those seven years of buying.

Most items are described fully below. I would like to point out the Easter basket in the bottom row. Those of you who were youngsters in this era (as I was) might wonder if your baskets were "MIOJ".

All items are marked "MIOJ" in red or black unless noted.

Top Row:

Boot, 2⅞"	$ 5.00-6.00
Lady's slipper, 2¾", "Pico"	6.00-7.50
Shoe, 2¾"	3.00-3.50
Shoe house, 4"	10.00-12.50
Baby shoe, 3⅝" x 2⅜", "Pico"	6.00-7.50
Brown and white shoe, 3"	3.00-3.50
Shoe, 2½", souvenir of a Mass. beach	4.00-5.00
"Wedgwood"-type vase, 3⅛"	6.00-7.50

Second Row:

Water sprinkling can, 2¾"	2.50-3.00
Wheelbarrow, 3½"	3.00-3.50
Shoe, 3½"	4.00-5.00
Pitcher vase, 3⅛"	2.50-3.00
Valise, 2⅛"	3.00-3.50
Pitcher, 3½"	8.00-10.00
Basket, 3"	5.00-6.00
Wooden rickshaw, 3½"	15.00-17.50
Pitcher vase, 3½", "Mariyama"	8.00-10.00

Third Row:

Blue pitcher, 2½", "Pico"	3.00-3.50
Pitcher, 2½"	2.50-3.00
Teapot and lid, 2¼"	4.00-5.00
Wells, 1⅜"	ea. 2.50-3.00
Bambo house, 2½"	6.00-7.50
Lighthouse, 2⅝"	2.50-3.00
Horse-drawn wagon, 4"	6.00-7.50
Car, 5"	10.00-12.50
Goose and basket, 1¾", "Pico"	4.00-5.00

Fourth Row:

All of this row except mermaid, castle and cat were part of a fish bowl assortment. Some pieces were only marked "Japan", but were all purchased at one time years ago. Price small items $2.00 to $3.00 and larger $4.00 to $5.00 each.

Mermaid, 3½" bisque	22.50-25.00
Castle, 3½" x 5½"	12.50-15.00
Cat w/fish, 4¼", bisque, for hanging on side of fishbowl	17.50-20.00

Row 5:

Covered urn, 2½"	6.00-7.50
Leaf, 2½", "Shofu China"	4.00-5.00
Egg cup, 2¼"	7.50-9.00
Pitcher, 3¼"	3.00-3.50
Wheelbarrow, 2", "H. Kato"	2.50-3.00
Easter basket, 7" x 7", marked in purple ink	30.00-35.00
Flower pot, 4½"	8.00-10.00
Vase, 2"	2.50-3.00
Pitcher, 2½"	3.00-3.50
Souvenir pitcher, 2½", "Francomb Notch, White Mts., N.H."	3.00-3.50
Souvenir pitcher, 3", "Singing Tower, Lake Wales, Fla."	3.00-3.50

PAPER, WOOD, ETC.

The items found here are some of the harder to find items that are "MIOJ". These, for the most part, were "disposable" and not intended to be kept. I can understand some girl keeping the party favor from the 1952 Junior/Senior banquet, but what story lies behind its suddenly finding its way onto today's collectible market?

I would like to point out the bowl in the lower right corner. It is made entirely of string wound tightly and glued together. Even the applied flowers are made of string. It looks like someone's craft project, perhaps "string art".

Top Row:	
Umbrella, 18″ before opening, "MIOJ" stamped on metal tip	$ 25.00-27.50
Umbrella, 22″ before opening, "MIOJ" stamped on metal tip	27.50-30.00
Second Row:	
Party horns, 12¼″	6.00-7.50
Paper lantern, 4¼″	10.00-12.50
"Bestmaid" needles, "50 asst. gold/silver eye needles w/threader, nickel plated, rust proof"	15.00-17.50
Third Row:	
Orange fan, 7¾″ spine	10.00-12.50
Blue fan, 8¾″ spine	12.50-15.00
Party favor, foldout flower, marked "Junior/Senior banquet, Apr. 27, 1951"	12.50-15.00
Fourth Row:	
Satin flower bunch	12.50-15.00
Pink and blue fan, 8½″ spine	10.00-12.50
Fan, 13¼″, silk-like cloth, wood handle	25.00-30.00
Pink flower bunch, 8½″, paper label	8.00-10.00
White w/flowers fan, 8½″	15.00-17.50
Fifth Row:	
Pink poseys, 4¼″, paper label	7.50-8.00
Flag, 1⅞″ x 1½″, silk, paper label, 48 stars, 3½″ tall	4.00-5.00
"Holiday" needle assortment	10.00-12.50
Party foldout, 6″	6.00-7.50
String bowl, 5¾″, paper label	20.00-25.00

PLANTERS - ANIMALS

I have to admit that these are among my least favorites in "OJ".

Thankfully, there are a few of these planters which will make you take note. The very first one in the top row really fooled me. It looks new, like the "Lefton China" you can buy in today's gift shops. It is "Lefton China" which is marked "MIOJ"! I have looked at several hundred pieces of "Lefton" since finding this swan and have not found another piece.

Some of the planters shown are more detailed than others, especially the small birds and ducks. Due to the popularity of collecting flamingos now, you had better catch a few before they take flight.

All items are marked "MIOJ" in black or red unless noted.

Top Row:
Swan, 4″ x 5½″ bisque, "Lefton China"	$ 20.00-25.00
Duck, 3½″ x 6″ (green)	12.50-15.00
Duck, 3″ x 5″ (green)	10.00-12.50

Second Row:
Goose, 3½″	5.00-6.00
Bird on tree branch, 3″	12.50-15.00 ea.
Rooster w/cart, 3″ x 4½″ (brown)	6.00-7.50
Birds in tree, 3¼″ x 4½″ (blue)	15.00-17.50

Third Row:
Duck w/scarf, 3¼″ x 4″	8.00-10.00
Owl, 2½″	8.00-10.00
Swan, 2″	3.00-3.50
Duck w/cart, 3″ x 5″	6.00-7.50
Donald duck, 3″	12.50-15.00

Fourth Row:
Swan, 3″ (blue)	5.00-6.00
Parrot, 6¼″	18.00-20.00
Duck w/hat, 6½″ x 6″ (blue)	10.00-12.50
Duck held by child, 4″	12.50-15.00

Fifth Row:
Bird w/house, 3″	6.00-7.50
Birds on flowers of branch, 3½″ x 4½″ (green)	12.50-15.00 ea.
Flamingo, 3″	15.00-17.50

PLANTERS - ANIMALS (Con't.)

There are pig and elephant item collectors who help decrease the supply of those particular animals. My Mother collects rabbits; her friend collects mice figures. So certain animal planters will sell. The smaller types are often used as toothpick holders.

If you would like to start collecting some "OJ" without a lot of competition, I would suggest planters or metallic objects. They are plentiful and usually inexpensive. Their variety seems endless. There are collectors for them. They just don't happen to be my favorites!

All items marked "MIOJ" in black or red unless noted.

Top Row:	
Rabbit w/cart, 2½" x 6"	$ 12.50-15.00
Elephant, 2" yellow	6.00-7.50
Elephant, 3½" x 5"	12.50-15.00
Pig, 2"	6.00-7.50
Lamb, 3"	5.00-6.00
Second Row:	
Monkey clown, 3¾"	8.00-10.00
Rabbit w/cart, 4" x 4"	12.50-15.00
Zebra, 5¼" x 6¼"	12.50-15.00
Ox w/cart, 2½" x 7"	8.00-10.00
Third Row:	
Donkey, 2¾"	6.00-7.50
Dog w/cart, 1¾" x 4"	4.00-5.00
Dog, 2⅞"	4.00-5.00
Dog w/shoe, 2"	6.00-7.50
Dog w/basket, 2", "Pico"	4.00-5.00
Fourth Row:	
Frog, 2¼"	8.00-10.00
Dog, 4¾"	12.50-15.00
Dog w/master, 5"	12.50-15.00
Dog, 4" x 6½"	10.00-12.50
Bear on log, 3½"	6.00-7.50
Fifth Row:	
Cat w/slipper, 2½" x 5¼"	10.00-12.50
Dog, 2¾"	3.00-4.00
Cow, 3" x 4"	8.00-10.00
Bug with bonnet, 4" x 4½"	10.00-12.50

PLANTERS — PEOPLE

Planters depicting people are not any more popular than those of animals, but those which show Orientals or exhibit quality workmanship sell better than the others. One of the things I pointed out in my previous books was that many of the figures came in several sizes. This is exhibited in the top row by the Oriental girl with fan. I am sure that there is a 6″ man to go with the girl as there is with the 4″ pair. There may even be 8″ examples of this pair. I have seen at least three different sizes of several similar figures.

The dancers in Row 2 are not commonly found and have some desirability with collectors. I am sure that there are several of those shown that are parts of sets. It seems to be more difficult to find planters in pairs than it is to find paired figurines.

The girl in the white dress in Row 4 was one of those pieces that did not look to be "OJ" when I first saw it. After a while, you learn to recognize "OJ" pieces before you ever pick them up to look for a mark. You will be fooled at times, as I was by the girl.

All items are marked "MIOJ" in black or red unless noted.

Top Row:

Boy at cactus, 4″	$ 6.00-7.50
Girl w/fan, 6″	12.50-15.00
Chinese pair of planters, 5″	10.00 ea. or 22.50-25.00 pr.
Seated Oriental, 4″	7.50-9.00

Second Row:

Dancers, 4½″	12.50-15.00 ea.
Colonial lady, 4″	5.00-6.00
Oriental lady head, 4″	10.00-12.50
Girl pushing cart, 4″	10.00-12.50

Third Row:

Boy w/bird, 3″	5.00-6.00
Couple, 2½″	8.00-10.00
Boy w/flowers, 2″	3.00-4.00
Boy w/horn, 3″	8.00-10.00
Boy w/guitar, 2¾″	6.00-8.00
Dutch girl w/cart, 2¾″	8.00-10.00

Fourth Row:

Girl w/white dress, 7″ (green)	18.00-20.00
Boy w/hat, 5½″	10.00-12.50
Coolie w/basket, 6″	10.00-12.50
Elf w/cart, 7½″, embossed "MIOJ"	15.00-20.00
Oriental, 5½″	15.00-17.50

Fifth Row:

Mexican w/guitar, 4¼″	12.50-15.00
Sleepy Mexican, 3½″	10.00-12.50
Mandolin player, 4″	6.00-8.00
Boy w/topknot, 4″	12.50-15.00
Girl w/basket, 4¾″	10.00-12.50

PLAQUES

Just when you think you have seen every type of plaque available in "OJ", along comes something new. That is how I felt when I saw the monkeys. There may be another to make the set, but two were entertaining enough for now. If you happen to have another to the set, let me know.

Although the first pair in the top row was purchased as a set and is marked with the same marking, you will note that the pieces are different. For photography purposes I am glad to have two different poses available, but it may be a different story when it comes time to sell them!

The Dutch boy in the middle row has a mate shown in a previous book; but this one is painted differently. All of the other plaques are bisque, but the Dutch boy is a type of chalkware.

All items are marked "MIOJ" in black or red unless noted.

Top Row;
Colonial couple, 6½" x 6" bisque, "Paulux" (1¼" thick) $ 42.50-45.00
Same as above only painted differently   42.50-45.00
Colonial lady, 7" x 4¾" bisque   27.50-30.00

Second Row:
Colonial couple, 6½" x 5¾", bisque   35.00 ea. or 72.50-75.00   pr.
Dutch chalkware boy, 7½", "Yomake"   20.00-22.50

Third Row:
Couple w/baskets, 6⅞" x 4¾", bisque, "Chase"   45.00 ea. or 95.00-100.00   pr.
Monkeys, 5", bisque, possible part of three-part set of
    "See, do or hear no evil"   32.50-35.00   ea.

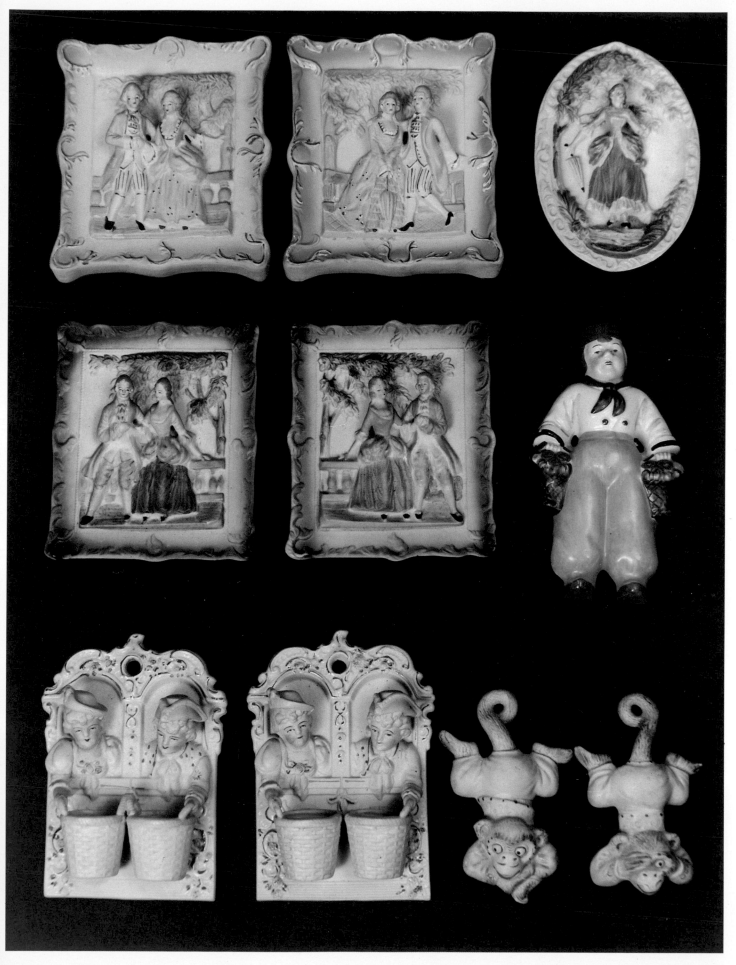

RUGS

The woven rug shown below is 3' x 5'. I bought it from a dealer at an antique show who said she would rip off the tag and sell it as an Applachian hooked rug if I did not buy it for my book! I saved it from that fate.

Unfortunately, you can only see half of the 9' x 12' rug on the opposite page at the top. The other half is the same but you miss the full effect. This is a room-size rug and is the largest I can confirm in existence. It was found at a flea market in conjunction with a sheep dog trial here in Lexington several years ago.

The bottom rug on the opposite page is 4' x 6' and does not have much history on its cloth tag. The frayed edges show someone used it. Except for the frayed edge and some missing fringe, the basic rug is still in good shape.

Bottom Page:
Woven rug, 3' x 5', #2000, "Mfg. by Franklin Rug Co.,
   Inc. N.Y., "MIOJ" $ 50.00-60.00

Opposite Page
Top: Wool hooked rug, 9' x 12', "Golden Gate, Design
   0818"   300.00-400.00
Bottom: Wool hooked rug, 4' x 6', cloth tag "MIOJ"   100.00-125.00

SALT and PEPPER SHAKERS

Collecting salt and pepper shakers has grown to such proportions that there are now several books devoted to them. Many of our "MIOJ" were included in these salt and pepper collections before "OJ" collecting came into being.

In my first book, I borrowed many shakers from my Mom's collection. She still collects shakers and I have borrowed some others from her for this book. Her large egg shakers in the top row are the only shakers that I have seen in two sizes. The larger eggs stand 5¾" tall while the smaller eggs are 3". Each egg fits into its own set of legs, with the egg being the shaker part.

The Black mammy and pappy are highly collectible even when not marked "OJ". You might recognize the Indians in the canoe from the Ethnic page, or at least one of them.

I might point out that many of the three pieced sets are not marked "OJ" except on the base piece. Usually the shaker parts of these sets say only "Japan" as there is not room for the word "Occupied". There are many shakers still being found in their original boxes with the boxes marked "MIOJ"; but the shakers are only marked "Japan". If the boxes are discarded, you lose the proof that they are truly "OJ".

All items are marked "MIOJ" in black or red unless noted.

Top Row:

Humpty Dumpty pair, "Ardalt, Lenwile China" No. 6343	$ 40.00-50.00
Humpty Dumpty pair, small, marked as above but No. 6577	27.50-30.00
Mammy and Pappy	35.00-40.00

Second Row:

Chicks in basket	20.00-22.50
"Hummel" type children in box marked "No. 150 c/mt 1 pair"	15.00-17.50
Chickens in basket	20.00-22.50
Mammy and Pappy	35.00-40.00

Third Row:

Pigs	15.00-17.50
Pigs in sty	20.00-22.50
Dogs	12.50-15.00
Southern belles	12.50-15.00

Fourth Row:

Indians	15.00-17.50
Indians in canoe	22.50-25.00
Fat boy single	6.00-7.50
Boy w/suspenders single	6.00-7.50
Duck hugger single	7.00-8.50

Fifth Row:

Corn cobs	10.00-12.50
Deer	12.50-15.00
Blue pitchers on tray	20.00-22.50

Sixth Row:

1st, 2nd and 9th, 10th Geese pairs	15.00-17.50 ea. pr.
3rd and 4th Ducks	10.00-12.50
5th, 6th Ducks and 7th, 8th Geese pairs	12.50-15.00 ea. pr.

SALT and PEPPER SHAKERS (Con't.)

There are several pairs of shakers shown here that would be prized by collectors other than "OJ" collectors. In Row 1, the baseball players have additional seekers in people who collect baseball memorabilia. They are avid collectors in their own right; it is a bonus to find an item that is sought by different fields of collecting. Not only could this be considered what is known as a "double" collectible, but it is a "triple" collectible. If you are a dealer, you can not find an item better than that for resale!

In the top row is an Oriental couple, each holding a pumpkin. They were purchased this way in a collection. I suspect that there are a couple of pumpkins missing and each is supposed to have two. That is only a guess on my part so if anyone out there knows for sure, I would like to know.

In the middle of Row 4 are strange looking children or maybe dwarfs. In the bottom row is a complete set; but the lady looses her head over the situation if you use the mustard or relish.

All items are marked "MIOJ" in black or red unless noted.

Top Row:

Baseball players (blue)	$ 20.00-22.50
Geisha girls	20.00-22.50
Bellhop w/suitcases	20.00-22.50
Coolies w/pumpkins	27.50-30.00

Second Row:

Graduates	18.00-20.00
Bride and groom	22.50-25.00
Scottish couple	15.00-17.50
Dutch girls	15.00-17.50

Third Row:

Indian zither players	15.00-17.50
Basket children, "Gaspe, P.Q."	20.00-22.50
Lily of Valley	12.50-15.00
Tea kettles	10.00-12.50
Tea kettle single, scenic	6.00-7.50

Fourth Row:

Cottage and lighthouse	22.50-25.00
Children w/animals	25.00-30.00
Glass shakers on tray, embossed in all three pieces	25.00-30.00

Fifth Row:

Glass on metal tray (tray marked also)	17.50-20.00
Metal shakers on tray (tray marked also)	15.00-17.50
Lady mustard and shakers, w/spoon and removable head	35.00-40.00

SETS - BEE, HOUSE and WINDMILLS

The toby set in the top row is reversible, e.g., it shows the same on both sides so it does not matter which way you set it down. It is the most interesting toby set I have ever seen including English ones.

The windmill set perhaps is missing a top to the creamer although most creamers do not have tops; this one seems to need one to complete the windmill. I have seen these pieces without the "OJ" markings frequently but very rarely with the "OJ" mark.

There are probably additional pieces to the windmill and the cottage sets. The bee pieces are desired by collectors of bee items without regard to their being "OJ".

All items are marked "MIOJ" in black or red unless noted.

Top Row:
Three-piece Toby set: sugar w/lid, creamer and individual teapot $ 75.00-90.00

Second Row:
Windmill, covered sugar, 4″	15.00-17.50
Windmill, creamer, 3″	8.00-10.00
Windmill, large salt, 3″	8.00-10.00
Windmill, teapot, 5″	35.00-40.00

Third Row:
Inside cottage scene, salt, pepper and marmalade on tray, "Maruhon Ware" with a K in circle mark	30.00-35.00
Windmill set, salt, pepper and mustard on tray	25.00-30.00
Inside cottage sugar w/lid, "Maruhon Ware" and K in circle	15.00-17.50

Fourth Row:
Cookie jar, 8″ x 6¼″, "Maruhon Ware"	65.00-75.00
Cottage grease or sugar	12.50-15.00
Biscuit jar, 6½″ x 5¼″	45.00-55.00

Fifth Row:
Bee creamer, 2½″	10.00-12.50
Bee teapot, 4½″	30.00-35.00
Bee sugar w/lid, 3½″	15.00-17.50

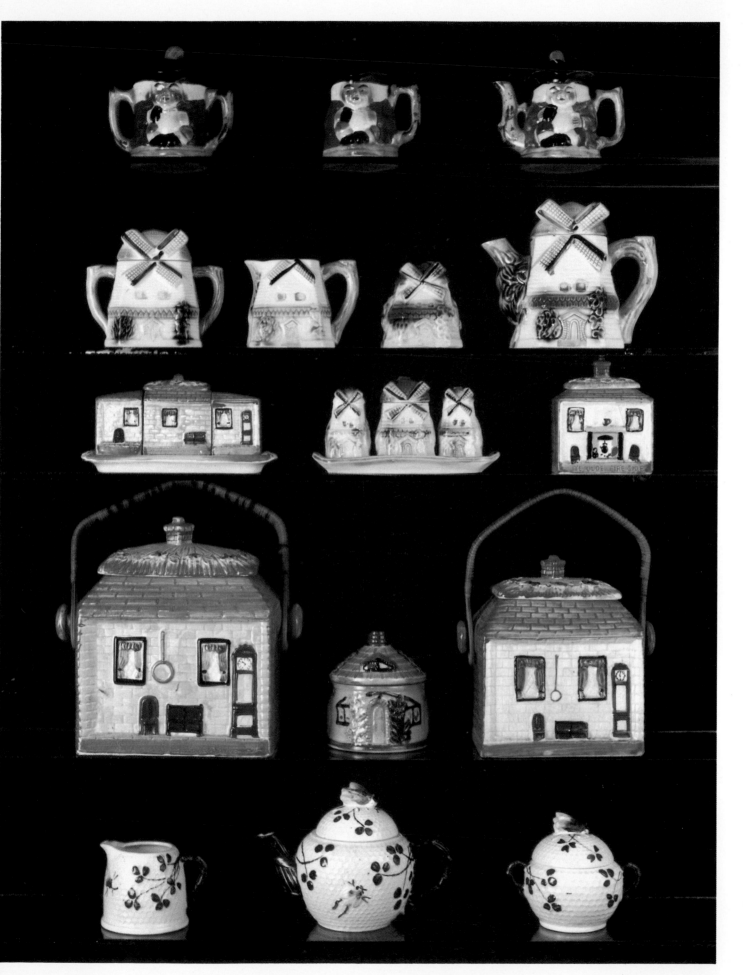

SETS - MISCELLANEOUS

In Rows 2 and 3 are examples of a serving set which was found in the Hawaii warehouse in the late 1970's. I have been told it was a rice or saki set. I will point out that the individual teapot is missing its lid. It was at the photography session in another box and not found until too late to include it. With over 2,000 pieces photographed in a couple of long days, some mistakes were inevitable.

The demitasse set on the wire rack is attractive; there are few sets found with the rack. The brown glaze teapots are all embossed on the bottom with "MIOJ". I have never seen anything else to go with these such as cups and saucers or a sugar and creamer.

All items are marked "MIOJ" in black or red unless noted.

Top Row:
Creamer, "Morikin Ware"	$ 8.00-10.00	
Rice bowl, 4", impressed mark	3.00-4.00	
Bowl, 3"	3.00-4.00	
Rice bowls, 4½" and 3½"	4.00-5.00	

Second Row:
Saki cups, 2¼"	6.00-7.50	ea.
3rd to 5th and all of Row 3 are samples of each piece of a serving set consisting of creamer, sugar w/lid, individual teapot, 8" shallow bowl, 7½" deep bowl, and four 4¼" small bowls	60.00-75.00	set

Fourth Row:
Demitasse set for six on rack, M on mountain scene mark	50.00-55.00	set
2nd, 3rd and 5th Saki cups, 2¼"	6.00-7.50	ea.
Teapot, 6½" x 9", brown	18.00-20.00	

SETS - STRAWBERRY and TOMATO

There are lots of tomato pieces available in both "OJ" and Japan. Actually, I have seen very few pieces with strawberries except for salt and pepper shakers which leads me to believe that the strawberry design is much rarer.

Note the three size tomato teapots. The cups or tumblers without handles are rarely found marked "OJ". In fact, they are rarely found at all. Those blue baskets' bases are the same except they have different fruits in each. You should be able to find additional pieces to both of these type sets. Let me know what pieces you find.

All items are marked "MIOJ" in black or red unless noted.

Top Row: STRAWBERRY
Strawberry sugar w/lid and creamer on tray, "Maruhon
   Ware" $ 25.00-27.50 set
Strawberry salt, pepper and mustard w/spoon in basket 27.50-30.00 set

Second Row - TOMATO:
Salt and pepper, 3½" 15.00-17.50
Salt and pepper, 3" 12.50-15.00
Sugar w/lid 12.50-15.00

Third Row - TOMATO:
Salt, pepper and mustard on tray 22.50-25.00 set
Teapot, 3", "Maruhon Ware" 30.00-35.00
Tumbler, 3", "Maruhon Ware" 10.00-12.50

Fourth Row - TOMATO:
Teapot, 4½", "Maruhon Ware" 40.00-45.00
Teapot, 5½", "Maruhon Ware" 50.00-55.00
Tumbler as in Row 3

Fifth Row - TOMATO:
Tumbler as in Row 3
Sugar w/lid and creamer on tray, "Maruhon Ware" 25.00-27.50
Salt, pepper and mustard w/spoon in basket 27.50-30.00 set

SHELF SITTERS and RECLINERS

I mentioned not having been able to find fishing poles for my shelf sitters in the last book. Several hundred bisque shelf sitters discovered in a warehouse in Georgia provided me with poles and several details which were new to me. They were packed in boxes of a dozen on benches which fit into the figure so that they would sit upright sturdily. I often wondered how these had survived all this time. We have had a difficult time in getting these to sit on the shelf edge when photographing. Any sudden movement or jar and disaster is imminent.

The first couple on Row 2 is made of unglazed pottery. These have almost a chalk feel and are extremely soft, which leads me to believe that few have made it into the 1980's. There are wall plaques made in this material and a few other items.

As in other cases, there is a premium price to be paid for pairs due to breakage over the years which has diminished the supply. I have to admit to a curiosity as to what the boy which matches the girl with the doll on the bottom row might be holding.

Top Row:

Accordian boy, 4″	$ 12.50-15.00	ea.
Girl w/bucket, 3″	10.00-12.50	
Oriental pr., 2¾″	12.50 ea. or 27.50-30.00	pr.
Fishing couple, 2½″, bisque with bisque fish on line	15.00-17.50	

Second Row:

Musicians, unglazed pottery, 4½″	12.50 ea. or 27.50-30.00	pr.
Oriental musicians, 5″	15.00 ea. or 30.00-35.00	pr.
Fishing couple on bench, 4″, bisque	17.50-20.00	
Fishing couple on bench, 2¼″, bisque	10.00-12.50	

Third Row:

Boy with basket, 4″	12.50-15.00	
2nd and 4th Oriental pair, 3″	8.50 ea. or 17.50-20.00	pr.
3rd and 5th Oriental pair, 3¼″	10.00 ea. or 20.00-22.50	pr.
Cowboy couple, 3½″ and 3¾″	12.50 ea. or 27.50-30.00	pr.
Colonial musicians, 3¼″	11.00 ea. or 22.50-25.00	pr.

Fourth Row:

1st and 6th Angels, 3″, bisque, "Lamore China"	20.00 ea. or 42.50-45.00	pr.
Girl and doll, 5″	17.50-20.00	
Fishing boy, 6½″, bisque	22.50-25.00	
Ballerina, 5″, net dress	22.50-25.00	
Mandolin player, 4″	12.50-15.00	

TEA SETS

The tea set at the top is not only a tea set but part of a dinnerware set. A reader of the first book noticed that we collected "Wild Rose" pattern by Fuji and wrote us about the teapot, creamer and sugar that she wished to sell. It made my wife very happy because we were using a creamer and sugar that were similar to "Wild Rose". I placed the rest of the dinnerware here rather than in the dinnerware section.

The blue "Noritake" set is one of the most exquisite tea sets I have ever seen that is "MIOJ". The teapot, creamer and sugar all have the same flower on them. Note how the flower and stems continue onto the lids of the sugar and teapot. The six cup and saucers each contain a different flower. I always meant to show them to a flower expert to identify them but never seemed to get around to it before it was too late for the book. I recognize the Tiger Lily, Orchid and Shasta Daisy, but the others are not in my flower reportoire.

Row 1 and Row 2 are "Wild Rose China" by "Fuji China"
Tea set consisting of teapot, creamer and sugar w/lid
and six cup and saucers. $135.00-150.00 set
Dinnerware set for eight consisting of 6¾" bread and
butter, 7½" salad and 10" dinner plates; 5½" cereal
and 6½" soup bowls; cup and saucers, creamer, sugar
w/lid and serving pieces as shown under "Dinner-
ware" on pages 50-57.   325.00-350.00

Row 3 and Row 4 are "Noritake"
Demitasse set consisting of demitasse pot, creamer and
sugar w/lid and six different cup and saucers.   150.00-175.00 set

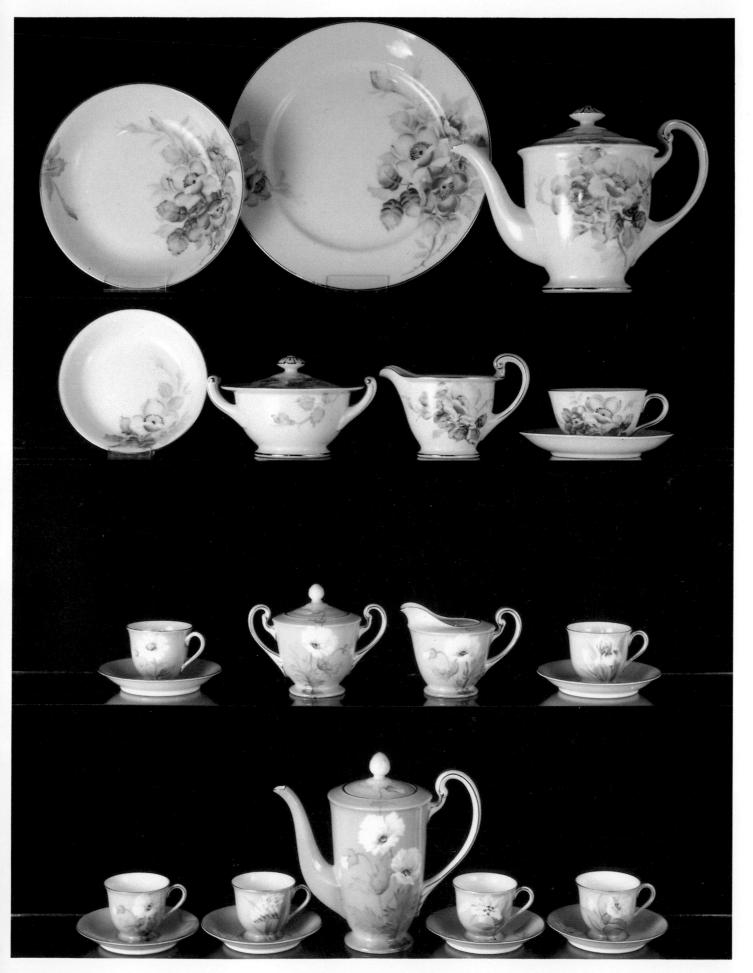

TOBIES and OTHER MUGS

Toby mugs have been collected for years, especially in England where Royal Doulton signals a quality-made item. The "OJ" tobies run the gamut from cheap imitations of the English-made wares to a few made of quality materials. The later ones are few and far between.

Since there are quite a few toby collectors, the competition for those "MIOJ" makes for a lively market in tobies. If you see several tobies in these styles, many will only be marked Japan. Evidently, there were many shipped into this country after the Occupation. This will also attest to their popularity.

Those large Father cups in the bottom row were Father's Day gifts according to people who had owned one. They will ensure you of a huge dose of caffeine in the morning.

All items are marked "MIOJ" in black or red unless noted.

Top Row:

Winker, 4″	$ 22.50-25.00
Barrel, 4¼″	10.00-12.00
Cannibal handled mug, 4¼″	32.50-35.00

Second Row:

Bearded man, 2¾″	17.50-20.00
Colonial man, 2¾″	15.00-17.50
3rd and 5th Colonial lady, 2″	12.50 ea. or 27.50-30.00 pr.
Old man, 1¾″	12.50-15.00
Lady w/basket, 2¼″	12.50-15.00
Lady w/fork, 2¾″	15.00-17.50
Red bearded man, 2⅞″, marked "MS" in shield	17.50-20.00

Third Row:

1st and 2nd Scarf lady, 2½″ possibly sugar and creamer	35.00-37.50 pr.
3rd Mustache man, 2¼″	25.00-27.50
4th and 6th Lady, 2½″	17.50-20.00
5th Colonial man, 3¼″	20.00-22.50

Fourth Row:

Stein, 6¾″	17.50-20.00
Stein, 7⅛″, "Bei trunk und scherz"	20.00-22.50
Bearded man, 4″	25.00-27.50

Fifth Row:

Father cup and saucer set, marked, "I bet you can't".	25.00-27.50 ea.

TOYS

My experience with toy collectors is that they will pay more for toys that are marked "OJ" than most "OJ" collectors will pay for the same item. It is not that they pay more because it is "MIOJ" but because it is a toy. In attending shows where toy dealers are displaying their stock, I have checked their prices on items that are marked or not marked. There is no difference in the price for the same item which means that "MIOJ" has little significance to them.

Most of the toys below came from the stock of a store that had been closed for quite a while in Georgia. I believe the explanations and descriptions below will suffice except for one observation about the sharp shooter. I always wondered why all the guns on this soldier were always broken off. After buying this one in the original box, I found out the reason. The end of the gun is rubber and it folds to fit the box since it is that much longer than the box. This makes a very weak spot in the gun which breaks off with a little use.

All items are marked on box as well as on the items themselves.

Top Row:
"Horse and Cart", "Trade Mark Modern Toys" $ 35.00-40.00

Second Row:
"Singing Chicken", "Trade Mark Modern Toys"   22.50-25.00
"Sharp Shooter", "Trade Mark Alps"   45.00-50.00

Third Row:
"Circus Bear", "Pat. #5309, Trade Mark, Tokyo"   45.00-50.00
"Kangaroo"   25.00-30.00
"Shimmy Donkey", "Registered #242160, Trade Mark
   Alps"   30.00-35.00

Fourth Row:
"Lucky Sledge", "(Oh Wonderful!), Kenkosha Toys In-
   dustrial Co., Inc., No. 806"   25.00-30.00
"Teddy's Cycle", "No. 501"   35.00-40.00
"Fancy Dan, The Juggling Man", "P. Patent #91688,
   Trade Mark, Modern Toys"   35.00-40.00

TOYS (Con't.)

The original box adds $5.00 to $7.50 to the value of the toys; so subtract that much if the box is missing. That goes for those on the previous page also.

I found the bamboo snake in Row 3 to be a fascinating item. It has a red tongue and twists and bends as well as any play snake I have seen except a rubber one. The hula girl has suction cups for feet so she probably was a dashboard ornament for the car. She really does shimmy well!

The tool set in the bottom row is my favorite. Each of the individual tools is embossed in the rubber part with "MIOJ" as well as the card which is stamped in purple ink. Would that all "MIOJ" items were marked so assiduously!

I am not sure whether the cigars explode or just sparkle. I am not brave enough to try one to see!

All items are marked "MIOJ" and boxes are also marked.

Top Row:
"Playful Little Dog"	$ 20.00-25.00	
"Hurricane Racer", "Trade Mark, KSG"	30.00-35.00	
"Champion", "Pat #PN05564, Sonsco", 29¢ price sticker	30.00-35.00	

Second Row:
"Singing Canary", "Trade Mark Alps, Pat. Pending, 'Wind the Spring and Watch ME Sing' "	30.00-35.00	
"Walking Bear"	20.00-25.00	
Penguin	17.50-20.00	
"My Favorite Watch" (hands moveable), card and watch both "MIOJ"	8.00-10.00	

Third Row:
"Stem Winding Watch", "#859", cardboard label on each watch, movie star pictures on each watch	3.00-4.00	ea.
"Ice Cream Vendor", "#660"	35.00-40.00	
Bamboo snake, 15½″	20.00-22.50	
Rabbit, cloth tag	18.00-20.00	
"Hula" dancer, "Okabe"	35.00-40.00	

Fourth Row:
"Ruby" watch, 1,2,3,6,9 dial	6.00-7.50	
"Special" cigar, (fireworks)	8.00-10.00	ea.
Tool set, 6 rubber pieces marked as well as card	40.00-50.00	
Dog (losing fur)	18.00-20.00	

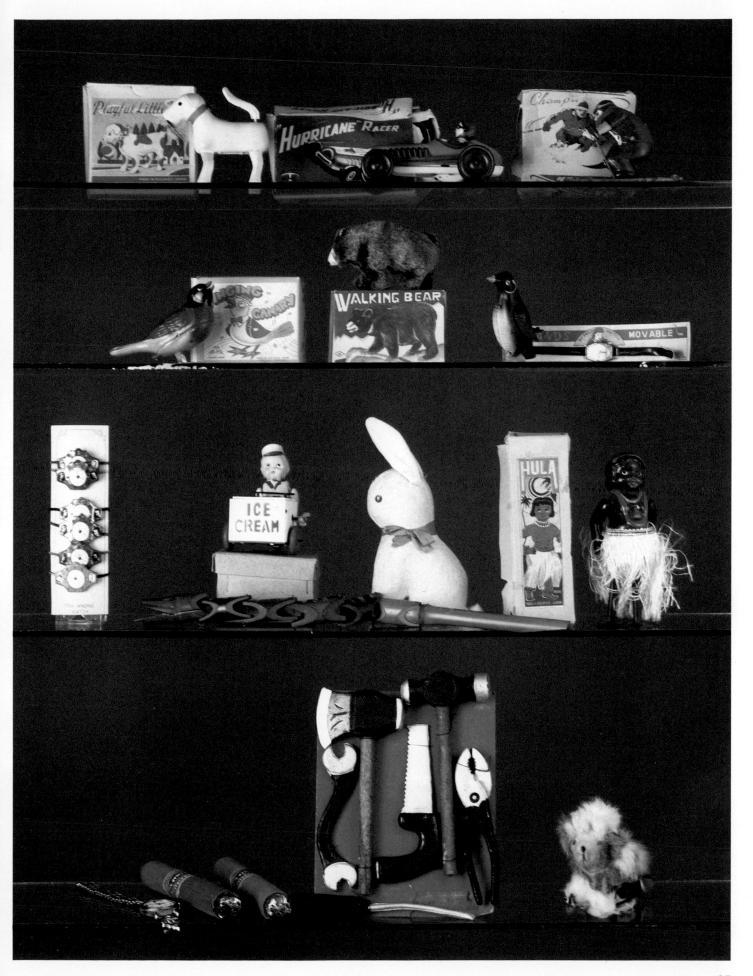

VASES

As you can see from these fifty vases, there is quite a variety available. There are small, cheaply made ones and some that are large and well made. The prices below will tell you that story.

In the top row the ballerina is quite unusual and the vase next to it with flowers in relief has some characteristics of Italy's famous Capo-Di-Monte.

In Row 2 are two smaller bisque vases (6th and 7th) with relief detail. They are only 4″ tall but are quite well made. In Row 3 there are two "Wedgwood"-type vases (4th and 6th) with chariot scenes. These are copies of the English pottery.

You might be able to see the embossed cat faces on the sides of the 8th vase in the bottom row if you look closely. This is bone china.

All items marked "MIOJ" in black or red unless noted.

Top Row:

Brown, 4¼″	$ 6.00-7.50
White, 4¾″, "Andrea"	15.00-17.50
Swan, 5″	10.00-12.50
Ballerina, 8¼″	50.00-60.00
Flowers in relief, 10⅛″	50.00-60.00
Blue and white, 8¼″	12.50-15.00
Boy ready for picnic, 5″	10.00-12.50

Second Row:

Dragon in relief, 2⅝″	8.00-10.00
Daffodil, 4″	6.00-7.50
Embossed flower, 5½″	6.00-7.50
4th and 5th, 2¼″ ea.	4.00-5.00
Bisque, 4″, "Morirama"	15.00-17.50
Bisque, 4″, "Morirama"	15.00-17.50
Swan, 5″	10.00-12.50
9th and 10th "Wedgwood"-type, 2⅝″ and bird in relief, 4″ ea.	8.00-10.00
Dragon, 2½″	4.00-5.00

Third Row:

Tulip, 2⅜″,	4.00-5.00
2nd and 9th, 3⅝″, "Pico"	5.00-6.00
Swan, 3¾″	10.00-12.50
"Wedgwood"-type, 6⅛″	40.00-50.00
Oriental man, 4¾″	17.50-20.00
"Wedgwood"-type, 6⅝″, "Ardalt"	50.00-60.00
Scenic, 3¾″	12.50-15.00
Floral, 4¼″, "Pico"	6.00-7.50

Fourth Row:

2¼″, "Pico"	4.00-5.00
2nd, 3rd and 9th 2¼″ to 2½″ ea.	2.50-3.00
4th, 6th and 10th 3″ and 2″ ea.	4.00-5.00
5th 3½″, "Moriyama"	4.00-5.00
7th Elf, 2½″, "Pico"	7.00-8.50
8th Wall pocket, flat side, 2½″, "Kukato"	6.00-7.50
11th Floral, 3″	6.00-7.50
12th Seated girl, 3½″, "EL" in cloud mark	10.00-12.50

Fifth Row:

1st "Wedgwood"-type, 2¾″	8.00-10.00
2nd and 11th 3″ and 2⅜″	4.00-5.00
3rd Pagoda in relief, 5¼″	20.00-22.50
4th, 7th and 9th 4½″ to 4¾″	12.50-15.00
5th Tulip, 4″, "Pico"	10.00-12.50
6th Green, 4″, "K" in circle mark	6.00-7.50
8th Cat faces embossed on sides, 5″, "Norleans Bone China"	20.00-22.50
10th Floral, 3″	5.00-6.00

LATE ARRIVALS

I have never written a book that after the photography was finished, some newly discovered pieces or an exciting new find didn't turn up almost immediately. As usual, I made room and time to include these pieces instead of waiting until the next book. There is a vast assortment, so the next few pages tell the never ending story this time.

I would like to point out one item that came from the Chief Paduke Flea Market in Paducah, Kentucky. The ice skating lady in Row 4, (6th item) my wife and I saw just after we had photographed the first session! Since it had some damage on it I convinced myself that I was not willing to buy it and hold it for the next book. Due to its being an unusual piece, I later regreted not purchasing it. Since several other pieces turned up including a dinnerware set in the two months from photographing to starting to write, I arranged another photography session on a Friday so I could go by the Flea Market and see if it was still there. It was! Of course all you ice skaters have never found yourself in this position!

All items are marked "MIOJ" in black unless noted.

Top Row:

Frog, 4½", bisque (29¢ marked on bottom)	$ 12.50-15.00	
Bowl, 7", octagonal, (red "G" in wreath)	12.50-15.00	
Plate, 8¼", "Rossetti, Chicago, USA"	22.50-25.00	
Horses, 7" tall	27.50-30.00	

Second Row:

Flamingo shakers, souvenir of Ft. Lauderdale, Fla.	12.50-15.00	
3rd and 6th Cowgirl and cowboy, 5½" (red "OJ")	12.50 ea. or 25.00-27.50	pr.
Calves, 4¾" (green)	10.00-12.50	ea.
Dutch shakers, 3½"	12.50-15.00	pr.

Third Row:

Tobies, 2¼", (reddish-orange)	15.00 ea. or 32.50-35.00	pr.
Bulldog, 4"	12.50-15.00	
Cow creamer, 8"	30.00-35.00	
Swan, 2¾"	4.00-5.00	
Vase, 2¾", amber glass, blue and white sticker	15.00-20.00	

Fourth Row:

Celluloid doll, 4½", embossed back	10.00-12.50
Doll, 2¾", impressed back (may have been in fire)	6.00-7.50
Lady w/flowers, 3½" (reddish-orange)	15.00-17.50
Wooden coaster, set of eight 2¾" in holder	17.50-20.00
Metal salt and pepper set, souvenir of Waterford Park	12.50-15.00
Tumbled ice skater, "Ardalt" #6350 (red)	25.00-30.00

Fifth Row:

Doll, 5¼", impressed mark	17.50-20.00	
2nd thru 5th Plaques, 4¼", "Ucagco China" (gold)	6.00 ea. or 25.00-30.00	set

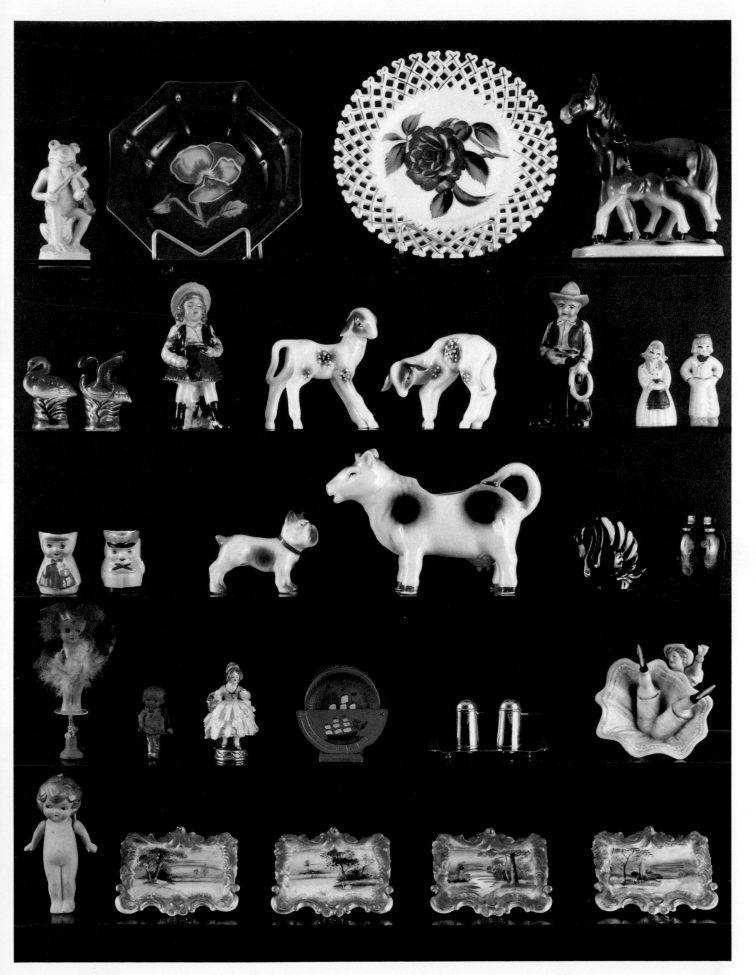

LATE ARRIVALS (Con't.)

Late is a good description for these! In fact I borrowed the third figurine couple in the bottom row a few hours before it was photographed. Right next to it is a seashell scene which was bought at the Stagecoach Antique Mall in Norwich, Ohio. It had come from Elizabeth Degenhart's house when the contents were sold in the fall of 1985. I will keep it as a souvenir due to its historical reminder and all the work I did on my book on Degenhart Glass.

The crystal lamps in the top row are among the finest examples of glass items that I have seen that were marked "MIOJ". They stand 8¾" tall to the top of the glass and 12" to top of the socket.

The basket in the middle row was purchased on the way to Paducah to the photography session. I offered to rent it and even sell it back the next day at the Nashville Flea Market at a loss. I still own it, and the antique mall I bought it from doesn't want it back!

Top Row:
1st and 4th Crystal lamps, 12" to socket, paper
   labels $ 70.00 ea. or 150.00-160.00   pr.
Lamp, 13" to socket, marked on porcelain under metal   30.00-32.50
Lamp, 10" to socket   35.00-40.00

Second Row:
1st and 3rd Bookends, heavy metal, 5¾" high   25.00-30.00   pr.
Basket, 10" "MIOJ" in purple   20.00-25.00

Third Row:
Man, 8½", bisque (red)   42.50-45.00
Man on fence, 7½", bisque (red)   35.00-37.50
Couple, 7¾" x 8½", bisque (ST in blue, "MIOJ")   200.00-225.00
Sea shell, 7" x 9", bisque "Ardalt #5157"   65.00-75.00

UNUSUAL ITEMS

The wooden box at the top of the next page was found several years ago in northern Ohio. It measures 14″ x 22″. It was shipped to "Wilder Trading Corporation, New York, New York", and contained twelve tins of 60 oz. "Canned White Meat Tuna Flakes", "Packed in Occupied Japan". I have had this for about six years and discussing it with collectors has brought only disbelief. Here it is! No other report of food containers has ever been confirmed to my knowledge. I have been offered the $100.00 at which it is valued.

The jewelry box shown closed at the bottom of the page was pictured open on page 75. It is 12″ x 5″ closed. The geisha girl dances when the box is opened. There is a paper blue and white "OJ" label on the bottom. $150.00-175.00

The record and the set pictured below were brought to me by Peggy and Chuck Nixon of Marietta, Georgia. I had heard of records, but never seen them. He even furnished the photographs to be included. You can read the name of the records in the set from the picture. The N-92 was missing from the set so if anyone out there has one let me know. Notice the set was $1.10 originally; but was bought at auction recently for $41.00. I guess that everyone can figure out that these are 78's.

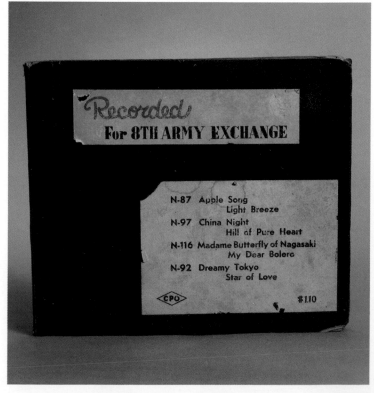

133

UNUSUAL (Con't.)

The vase shown below is the largest I have seen that is "MIOJ". It stands 13″ high and is 9½″ in diameter. It is Lacquerware marked in gold, "Mariyama, Patent, Made in Occupied Japan" with a globe inscribed in gold. There were probably words on the gold bands at one time, but they are not legible now. This may not end this book with as stirring a find as the first book's cuckoo clock, but it does not make as much noise as that cuckoo did either. As I close another book, may I wish health, happiness and happy collecting.

Vase Value $75.00-90.00

PRICE GUIDE FOR OCCUPIED JAPAN I

Page 8

Top Row:

Dogs	3.00-3.50
Pigs	5.00-6.00
Bees	6.50-7.00
Ducks	3.25-3.50

2nd Row:

Dogs	4.50-5.00
Bird	3.00-3.50
Receiving Set	3.50-4.00

3rd Row:

Dogs	7.00-8.00
Deer	3.50-4.00
Duck	5.50-6.00
Bird	3.00-3.50

4th Row:

Dogs	6.00-6.50
Birds	3.00-3.50
Lamb	2.50-3.00
Turtle	7.50-8.00
Bee	7.00-7.50

5th Row:

Dogs	9.50-10.00

Page 10

Top Row:

Bears	5.00-6.00
Dogs	5.00-6.00
Monkey Set	4.50-5.00

2nd Row:

Dog	6.50-7.50
(same dog as in top row, only larger)	
Horse	6.00-6.50
Pig	5.00-5.50
Peacocks	5.00-6.00
Mouse	5.00-5.50

3rd Row:

Cat	3.50-4.00
Cat Groups	7.50-8.50
Butterflies	7.50-8.50
Dog	3.00-3.50

4th Row:

Cats	4.50-5.00
Horse Drawn Planter	5.00-6.00
Ox Drawn Planter	4.50-5.00
Dog	6.00-6.50

5th Row:

Frog Ash Tray	10.00-12.50
Frog Vase	10.00-12.50
Fish	3.00-3.50
Peacock	5.00-6.50
Cat Pencil Holder	3.00-3.50

Page 12

Top Row:

Coal Bin and Tray	15.00-17.50
Elephant Set (5 Trays)	17.50-20.00

2nd Row:

Alligator	10.00-11.50
"Wedgwood" Types	5.50-6.50
Frog	10.00-12.50

3rd Row:

Dresser and Top	5.00-5.50
Cigarette Boxes (4 Trays)	15.00-17.50

4th Row:

Cigarette Box (4 Trays)	15.00-17.50
Ash Trays (Part of Sets Above)	2.50-3.00

Bottom:

Square Ash Tray	2.00-2.50
Rose Ash Tray	2.00-2.50
/Set of 4 and Box	15.00-17.50
Negro Holder	17.50-20.00

Queen of Hearts, Part of Set	3.00-3.50
Oriental Face, Part of Set	3.00-3.50
/Set w/box	12.50-15.00
Leaf	3.00-3.50
Rectangular Tray	3.00-3.50

Page 14

Top Row:

Rotating Cable Car, San Francisco	20.00-22.50
Horses, Lexington, Ky.	5.00-6.00

2nd Row:

St. Louis Zoo	2.50-3.00
Hollywood	2.50-3.00
Large Cowboy Tray	3.00-3.50

3rd Row:

Dog Cigarette or Jewel Box	8.50-9.50
St. Petersburg, Fla. Tray	2.50-3.00
Jewel Box	6.00-6.50
Double Tray	3.50-4.50
Cowboy Boot Lighter/Tray	12.50-15.00

4th Row:

Large Ash Tray	4.50-5.00
Small Tray	2.50-3.00
Devil Ash Tray	12.50-15.00

Bottom:

Silent Butler	10.00-12.50
Butter Dish (Glass Liner)	10.00-12.50
Florida Ash Tray	2.50-3.00
Cigarette Box/Ash Tray on Stand	15.00-17.50

Page 16

Top Row:

Cream Pitcher (Part of Tea Set)	8.00-9.00
Egg Cup (Part of Dinnerware Set)	12.50-15.00
Pitcher	4.50-5.00
Half Potty	3.00-3.50

2nd Row:

Book Ends	pr 20.00-22.50
Pitcher	7.50-8.50

3rd Row:

Stacking Set	ea 3.00
	set 12.50
Black Boy at Outhouse	20.00-22.50
Cup and Saucer	15.00-17.50
Dutch Girl Bell	12.50-15.00
Candle Holder	ea 12.50
	pr 25.00

Bottom:

Cornucopia Vase	4.50-5.00
Vase	4.00-4.50
Covered Powder Jar	7.50-10.00
Butt Snuffer	4.50-5.00
Pitcher	3.50-4.00
Vase	3.50-4.00

Page 18

Canisters	ea 15.00-17.50
	set 100.00-125.00

Page 20

Top Row:

Dancers, Working Key Wind	27.50-30.00
Non Working	12.50-15.00
Reindeer	10.00-12.50
Baby Rattle	15.00-17.50

2nd Row:

Baby Rattle	15.00-17.50
Dog	10.00-12.50
Doll, Movable Legs	15.00-17.50

3rd Row:

Pig (Tape Measure)	17.50-20.00
Doll (Bisque-Like)	15.00-17.50

Scotty Dog, Working Key Wind	27.50-30.00
Non Working	12.50-15.00

Bottom:

Composition Doll	17.50-19.50
Negro Doll, Mint w/Clothes	32.50-35.00
As Pictured	15.00-17.50
12" Doll, Mint	35.00-37.50
Some Damage	15.00-17.50
5" Doll, Mint	20.00-22.50
Some damage, as shown	10.00-12.50
Football Player	15.00-17.50

Page 22

Place Settings:

Two	17.50-20.00
Three	20.00-25.00
Four	30.00-35.00
Four w/Tureen and Platter	40.00-45.00
Five	45.00-55.00
Six	55.00-65.00

Page 24

Top Row:

Cup (Saucer?)	5.00-5.50
Demi-Set	10.00-12.50
Cherry China Sets	8.00-10.00
Hexagonal Demitasse Set	10.00-11.50

2nd Row:

1st and 4th Sets	6.00-7.00
2nd and 5th Demitasse Sets	10.00-12.00
Middle Set	9.50-10.00

3rd Row:

1st and 2nd Sets	8.00-9.00
3rd and 4th Sets	7.00-7.50
5th Cup	12.50-15.00

4th Row:

1st Demitasse Set	12.50-15.00
2nd and 4th Sets	8.00-10.00
Middle Set	12.00-15.00
5th Demitasse Set	5.00-6.00

5th Row:

1st Set	9.50-10.00
2nd and 4th Sets	10.00-11.50
Middle Set	15.00-17.50
5th Set, Souvenir Santa Claus, Ind.	12.00-13.50

Page 26

Top Row:

Plate "Noritake"	4.00-5.00

2nd Row:

Hexagonal Plate	3.00-3.50
2nd and 4th Plates	3.00-3.50
3rd Plate	7.00-8.00
5th Plate	2.00-2.50

3rd Row:

Plate, Souvenir of Oklahoma City, Okla.	4.00-5.00
2nd Plate w/Sailboat	7.00-7.50
Ohio Map	10.00-12.50
Celery	5.00-6.00

4th Row:

Violet Plate	12.00-13.50
Fruit Plate	10.00-12.50
Flower Plate	10.00-12.50

Bottom:

1st Plate	2.00-2.50
Bonbon Tray	7.50-8.50
Flower Plate	6.00-7.50

Page 28

Cherry China

8 Place Setting w/Serving Pieces	150.00-200.00
12 Place Setting w/Serving Pieces	200.00-300.00

Noritake China
8 Place Setting w/Serving
Pieces 175.00-250.00
12 Place Setting w/Serving
Pieces 250.00-400.00

Page 30
Top Row:
Ship 9.00-10.00
Bisque Boy and Girl 17.50-20.00
Castle 5.00-6.00
Bisque Boy 12.50-15.00
2nd Row:
Castle 4.00-5.00
Cats 17.50-20.00
Goldfish 8.00-9.00
Bisque Boy and Girl 13.00-15.00
Bottom:
Castle Atop Bridge 7.00-8.00
Pagoda Bridge 8.00-9.00
Mermaid 17.50-20.00

Page 32
Top Row:
Blue Cologne and Tray 20.00-25.00
. . . . ea 12.50-15.00
2nd Row:
Perfume 20.00-22.50
Duck, w/Sticker 6.50-7.00
Pink Cologne or Perfume . . . 15.00-17.50
3rd Row:
Shakers 15.00-17.50
Dogs, w/Sticker . . . . set 30.00-32.50
Shakers, w/Stand . . . . pr 20.00-22.50
4th Row:
Sport Glasses 25.00
w/case 35.00
Ash Tray 12.00-15.00

Page 34
Lacquerware Lamp 30.00-35.00
Colonial Single 27.50-30.00
Colonial Single, sans Socket . 25.00-27.50
w/socket 32.50-35.00
Colonial Pair, Left 50.00-57.50
Pair Lamps, Right 50.00-57.50

Page 36
Plates 4.50-5.00
Coasters, 2 Sizes 2.50-3.00
Wall Shelf Unit 30.00-35.00
Lamp Base 25.00-27.50
Ice Bucket and Tongs 27.50-30.00
Salad Bowl w/Fork and
Spoon 20.00-22.50
Bowl w/6 Individual Bowls
and Spoon 25.00-30.00

Page 38
Top Row:
Lamp Lighter 15.00-17.50
Donkey Lighter 20.00-22.50
Boot Lighter 7.50-8.50
2nd Row:
Coat of Armor Lighter 15.00-17.50
Inlaid Lighter 12.00-15.00
Mint Compote 5.00-6.00
Table Gun Lighter 20.00-22.50
Shoe Pin Cushion 7.50-8.00
3rd Row:
Table Lighter 5.00-6.00
Gun Lighter 12.00-13.50
Bulldog Pencil Sharpener . . . 8.00-9.50
Shaker and Mustard Set
w/Tray 20.00-22.50
Trophies 2.00-2.50
Donkey Jewel Chest 15.00-17.50
Bottom:
Tea Holder 12.00-14.00
Nut Dish 5.00-5.50
Key Lighter 7.50-9.00
Pencil Lighter 15.00-17.50

Page 40
Top Row:
All Items Save 2nd Teapot . 3.00-3.50
2nd Teapot w/Removable
Lid 5.00-6.00
2nd Row:
All Items Save Half Potty
and Lookout Mt. Pitcher . 3.00-3.50
Half Potty 3.50-4.00
Lookout Mt. Pitcher 3.00-3.50
3rd Row:
All Items Save
Martha/George
and Floral Vase 2.50-3.00
Martha and George Set 12.00-14.00
Blue Floral Vase 6.50-7.50
4th Row:
All Items 3.50-4.00
5th Row:
All Items Save Small Trays
and Nude Boy 3.50-4.00
Nude Boy 4.00-4.50
Tray w/6 Pieces—
Removable Lid on Pitcher 17.50
Incomplete 2.00
Only the trays are marked
"Made in Occupied
Japan"

Page 42
Large Umbrella, Approx.
3 Ft. Across 25.00-27.50
Wood Jewelry Box 12.50-15.00
Camera, Self Developing
Film 75.00-80.00
Decorative Fan 6.00-7.00
Small Umbrellas 5.00-6.00
Christmas Ornament 12.00-14.00
Doll Chest 25.00-30.00
Box, Secret Opening 25.00-30.00
Ship (String and Wood) . . . 10.00-12.00
Santa on Sleigh 22.50-25.00
Rag Time Band, Boxed Set
($3.00 ea) 25.00-27.50

Page 44
Top Row:
All Items Save Bee 5.00-6.00
Bee 6.50-7.00
2nd Row:
All Items Save Rabbit 5.00-6.50
Rabbit 6.50-8.00
3rd Row:
All Items 5.00-6.50
4th Row:
Duck and Donkey 5.00-6.50
Boat 15.00-17.50
5th Row:
Donkey, Left 10.00-12.00
Donkey, Center 6.00-7.00
Zebra 7.00-9.00

Page 46
Top Row:
Small Girl 3.00-3.50
Oriental Heads 15.00-17.50
2nd Row:
1st and 4th Planters 7.50-9.00
2nd and 3rd
Planters/Bookends 12.50-15.00
3rd Row:
All Items 7.50-10.00
4th Row:
All Items Save Center
Pieces 6.00-8.00
Tall Center Pieces 13.50-15.00

Page 48
Top Row:
All Items Save Miniature
Toby Shakers 9.00-10.00

Toby 12.00-13.50
2nd Row:
All Items Save Martha and
George 9.00-10.00
Martha and George 15.00-17.50
3rd Row:
All Items Save Frogs 10.00-12.00
Frogs 15.00-17.50
4th Row:
Three Piece Sets 17.50-20.00
5th Row:
Three Piece Sets, Save
Cucumbers 17.50-20.00
Cucumbers 20.00-22.50

Page 50
Top Row:
Chicken and Girl 4.00-5.00
Boats/3 Piece Sets 15.00-17.50
Gaily Decorated 17.50-20.00
2nd Row:
4 Piece Metal Set 20.00-22.50
Glass Shakers and Metal
Stand 20.00-22.50
Hobnail Shakers 15.00-17.50
Frogs/3 Piece Set 15.00-17.50
Clown 7.50-8.50
3rd Row:
Tomato, Pr. 5.00-6.00
Tomato Sets on Leaf
w/Mustard 15.00-17.50
4th Row:
Blue/White Shakers
(Match egg cup pictured on
page 17) 15.00-17.50
Windmills w/Moving Blades 25.00-27.50
Negro Cooks, Pr. 30.00-32.50
Cottages and Peppers 8.00-9.00
Boy 5.00-6.00
5th Row:
Beehive Set 15.00-17.50
Beehive Sugar and
Marmalade 17.50-20.00
Separate Sugar 10.00-12.00
Ceramic Set on Tray 20.00-22.50

Page 52
Top Row:
Statue, Flat Gap, Ky. 15.00-17.50
Pitcher, Lookout Mt., Tenn. 3.50-4.00
Statue, Canadian National
Exhibition 12.00-14.00
2nd Row:
Toothpick, Wisconsin 3.50-4.00
Cats, Niagara Falls, Canada 8.00-10.00
Plate, Oklahoma City, Okla. 3.50-4.00
Vase, Canada 3.50-4.00
Cup and Saucer, Santa Claus,
Ind. 10.00-11.50
Pitchers, Mt. Vernon, Va. . . 9.00-10.00
3rd Row:
Tray, New York City 2.50-3.00
Tray, St. Louis Zoo 2.50-3.00
Tray, Catskill Mts. 2.50-3.00
4th Row:
Ash Tray, Lexington, Ky. . . 4.00-4.50
Map Dish, Ohio or Other
States 10.00-12.50
Ash Tray, San Francisco . . . 20.00-22.50

Page 54
Top Row:
Sugar, Left 15.00-17.50
Teapot, Sugar and Creamer . 50.00-57.50
Individual Teapot 15.00-17.50
2nd Row:
As Shown 60.00-65.00
3rd Row:
Creamer and Sugar 15.00-17.50
Teapot 17.50-20.00

Page 56
Top Row:
Tea Set 50.00-60.00
Middle:
Bowl 20.00-22.50
Square Flat Dish 12.00-12.50
Bottom:
Cup and Saucer Set w/Stand 40.00-50.00
Candy Dish 15.00-17.50
Page 58
Top Row:
All Toby Mugs 15.00-17.50
2nd Row:
All Toby Mugs Save 3rd
   from Left 15.00-17.50
3rd Toby Mug from Left . . . 17.50-20.00
3rd Row:
Tobies, Either End 17.50-20.00
Other Toby Mugs 15.00-17.50
4th Row:
Large Heads 17.50-20.00
Small Heads 10.00-12.00
5th Row:
1st Two Toby Mugs 13.50-15.00
3rd Toby 25.00-27.50
Barrel Mug 15.00-17.50
MacArthur Toby 35.00-40.00
Page 60
Top Row:
All Items 4.00-4.50
2nd Row:
All Items Save Liberated
   Girl 4.00-4.50
Topless Girl 8.00-10.00
3rd Row:
All Items, Save Naked Girl
   and Wagon 3.00-3.50
Naked Girl and Vase 8.00-9.00
Girl w/Wagon 9.00-10.00
4th Row:
All Items, Save Angel on
   Star 4.00-4.50
Angel on Shooting Star 8.00-10.00
5th Row:
All Items, Save Tree 6.00-8.00
Tree 4.50-5.00
Page 62
Top Row:
Dancing Elephant in Original
   Box 30.00-35.00
Dancing Bear in Original
   Box 25.00-30.00
Hopping Squirrel 25.00-30.00
2nd Row:
Running Mouse in Original
   Box 17.50-20.00
Wind Up Car 12.50-15.00
Baby Jeep in Box 12.50-15.00
3rd Row:
Car w/Box 12.50-15.00
Fly Pin on Card 4.50-5.00
Beetle 17.50-20.00
Watches on Card 10.00-12.50
Bottom:
Box of Puzzles
   w/Instructions 45.00-55.00
Page 64
Top Row: (Left to Right)
All Vases, Save 5th and 6th 4.00-6.00
5th Vase, Looks Like
   Egyptian Hieroglyphics . . 7.00-9.00
6th, Kutani-Type 5.00-6.00
2nd Row:
All Save 4th Pair 5.00-6.50
4th Pair, Kutani-Type 7.00-8.50
3rd Row:
Six Kutani-Types 5.50-6.50

2nd Vase 6.00-7.50
6th, 7th, 8th Vases 3.00-4.50
4th Row:
Six Kutani-Types 6.00-7.00
Others 3.00-3.50
Bottom:
All Vases 3.00-4.50
Page 66
Top Row:
All Vases 5.00-6.00
2nd Row:
All Vases Save 2nd and 5th 6.00-7.00
2nd Vase, Children 7.50-8.50
5th Vase, Seated Figure 17.50-20.00
3rd Row:
All Vases Save George
   Washington 5.00-6.00
George Washington 7.50-8.50
Bottom:
1st Vase, Fine Quality 20.00-22.50
Iris Vases 30.00-35.00
4th Vase, Enclosed Figure . . 20.00-22.50
5th Vase 10.00-12.50
Page 68
Top Row:
Elf on Praying Mantis 20.00-22.50
Angel 4.00-5.00
Middle:
Seated Elves with Planters . 15.00-17.50
Angel w/Flute 5.00-6.00
Bottom:
Seated Elf 12.00-14.00
Reclining Elf 12.00-14.00
Angel w/Sleeping Child 20.00-22.50
Standing Angel 5.00-6.00
Page 70
Top Row:
Peasant Girl Standing 15.00-17.50
Farmer w/Rake 15.00-17.50
M'Lady w/Dove 50.00-57.50
Peasant Boy 15.00-17.50
Seated Girl 20.00-22.50
Middle:
Man w/Cane 17.50-20.00
Boy w/Dog 20.00-22.50
Bottom:
Boy Holding Mug 17.50-22.50
Standing Lady w/Hat 17.50-20.00
Lad w/Cloak 17.50-20.00
Seated Little Boy 10.00-12.00
Standing Dowager 15.00-17.50
Peasant Lass 10.00-12.00
M'Lord Standing 20.00-22.50
Page 72
Top Row:
Boy and Girl Pair 50.00-60.00
2nd Row:
Seated Musician Pair 45.00-50.00
Plaques Pair, Mint 45.00-50.00
Boys Holding Leaves 32.50-35.00
3rd and 4th Row:
Girl and Boy on Left, Pr. . . . 35.00-37.50
Seated Boy and Girl 10.00-12.50
Japanese Pair 22.50-25.00
Man and Woman on Right,
   Pr. 40.00-45.00
Bottom:
All Seated Figures 12.00-15.00
Page 74:
Top Row:
All Items Save Center Boy
   w/Duck 6.00-7.00
Boy w/Duck 10.00-12.00
2nd Row:
All Items Save Reclining
   Girl 5.00-6.00
Reclining Girl w/Bird 7.00-8.00

3rd Row:
All Items 4.00-5.00
4th Row:
1st Five Items 5.00-6.00
Last Five Items 10.00-12.00
5th Row:
Boy and Dog, Left 17.50-20.00
Remaining Items 12.50-15.00
Page 76
Top Row:
All Items Save Clarinet
   Player & Drummer 5.00-6.00
Clarinet Player and Bisque
   Drummer 9.00-10.00
Middle:
All Items Save Small Figure
   in Front 7.00-9.00
Small Figure (Gabriel?) 4.00-4.50
Bottom:
All Items Save Last 5.00-6.00
Last Boy and Dog 12.00-14.00
Page 78
Top Row:
Shelf Sitters 10.00-12.00
Boy and Girl at Ends 5.00-6.00
Middle Two Girls 12.00-15.00
Middle:
Shelf Sitters 10.00-12.00
Boy and Girl in Center 5.00-6.00
Girl in White 3.00-4.00
Bottom:
Shelf Sitters 10.00-12.00
Tall Girl 5.00-6.00
Small Girl 5.00-6.00
Page 80
Top Row:
Ballerina 25.00-30.00
White Dress Dancer 15.00-17.50
Pink Dress Dancer 10.00-12.50
Lavender Dress Dancer 15.00-17.50
Middle:
Girl Ballerina and
   Green Dress Dancer 8.00-10.00
Tall Girl w/Hat 20.00-22.50
Bottom:
All Dancers 9.00-10.00
Page 82
Top Row:
Boy and Girl 12.50-15.00
2nd Row:
Colonial Man and Woman,
   Pr. 17.50-20.00
Pr., Middle Left 10.00-12.00
Center Pair 9.00-10.00
Pr., Middle Right 12.00-14.00
Colonial Man and Woman . . 20.00-22.50
Bottom:
Taller Couple 17.50-20.00
Center Pair 12.50-15.00
Couple at Right 17.50-20.00
Page 84
Top Row:
Lady Holding Hat 20.00-22.50
Dutch Sailor w/Bag 17.50-20.00
Middle:
Lady w/Feathered Hat 20.00-22.50
Lady Holding Hat 20.00-22.50
Bottom:
M'Lady w/Basket 25.00-27.50
Dutch Girl 17.50-20.00
Windmill Shakers 12.50-15.00
Windmill Shakers w/Turning
   Blades 25.00-27.50
Page 86
Top Row: (Left to Right)
1st, 2nd, 4th and 7th Couple 12.50-15.00
3rd Couple 5.00-6.00

5th Couple............	4.50-5.00
6th Group.............	17.50-20.00
2nd Row:	
1st, 2nd and 7th Couple....	12.50-15.00
3rd, 5th and 6th Couple....	5.50-6.50
4th, Bride and Groom.....	22.50-25.00
3rd Row:	
All Couples Save 6th......	12.50-15.00
6th Couple..............	5.50-6.00
4th Row:	
1st Couple, Fine Detail.....	22.50-25.00
2nd and 5th Couples.......	12.50-15.00
6th Couple, Canadian National Exposition Souvenir.....	12.00-14.00
3rd Couple.............	10.00-12.00
Bride and Groom.........	30.00-35.00
7th Couple.............	15.00-17.50
5th Row:	
Man Pushing Sleigh.......	42.50-45.00
2nd Couple............	27.50-30.00
3rd Couple............	32.50-35.00
4th Couple............	15.00-17.50

Page 88
Top Row:	
1st, 2nd and 5th Musicians.	5.50-6.50
3rd Figure............	12.50-15.00
4th Figure............	7.00-8.00
2nd Row:	
1st Figure.............	5.00-6.00
2nd Figure............	3.00-3.50
3rd Pair.............	8.00-10.00
4th Figure............	3.50-4.00
5th Figure............	8.00-10.00
3rd Row:	
1st and 2nd Figures......	5.00-6.00
Girl and Piano.........	15.00-17.50
Piano Ensemble..........	30.00-35.00
Man and Piano.........	17.50-30.00
4th Row:	
Seated Bisque Pair........	45.00-50.00
Organ Grinders..........	15.00-17.50
4th Man w/Fiddle.......	12.00-14.00
6th and 7th Foursome.....	25.00-30.00
5th Row:	
Maid w/Suitor..........	20.00-22.50
3rd and 4th, Men.......	12.50-15.00
Seated Flutist...........	12.50-15.00
End Pair Musicians........	20.00-25.00

Page 90
Top Row:	
Figures 1,3,5, and 6.......	6.00-7.00
Bisque Figures 2 and 8....	10.00-12.00
Reclining Figure.........	8.00-10.00
Small Girl #7..........	6.00-6.50
2nd Row:	
Figures 1 and 4..........	5.50-7.00
Rickshaw.............	17.50-20.00
Man w/Clay Pots.......	9.00-10.00
Shelf Sitter...........	10.00-12.00
3rd Row:	
Shelf Sitters...........	10.00-12.00
Figures 2,3,4,5, and 9......	6.00-7.00
Figure 6.............	4.00-4.50

Bisque Girl #7..........	12.00-14.00
4th Row:	
Girls 1 and 7, Fine Detail..	17.50-20.00
Figures 2,5, and 6........	15.00-17.50
3rd Figure...........	12.50-15.00
Tall Figure #4.........	27.50-30.00

Page 92
Top Row:	
Shelf Sitter...........	10.00-12.00
Figures 2 and 3........	5.50-6.00
Figures 4, 7 and 8.......	4.50-6.00
Incense burners.........	13.50-15.00
2nd Row:	
Figures 1,2,3..........	8.00-10.00
Figures 4 and 5, Pr.....	12.00-14.00
Figures 6 and 7.......	6.00-7.00
3rd Row:	
Rickshaw.............	17.50-20.00
Bookends.............	20.00-22.50
Figures 4 and 5, pr......	7.00-8.00
Bottom:	
Pair, Each End..........	25.00-27.50
Figures 3 and 4, ea......	12.00-14.00
Figures 5 and 6, pr.......	45.00-50.00

Page 94
Top Row:	
1st Pair.............	3.50-4.50
Pairs 2 and 5.........	7.50-9.50
3rd Pair.............	12.00-14.00
4th Pair.............	25.00-30.00
6th Pair.............	7.50-8.00
2nd Row:	
Pairs 1 and 5.........	15.00-17.50
Pairs 2 and 3.........	10.00-12.00
4th Pair.............	12.00-14.00
3rd Row:	
1st and 2nd Figures......	10.00-12.00
Pairs 3 and 4.........	22.50-25.00
Pairs 5 and 6.........	10.00-12.00
4th Row:	
Pairs 1 and 3, Nice Detail..	45.00-50.00
2nd Pair, Signed Andrea...	57.50-67.50

Page 96
Top Row:	
Baseball Player...........	8.00-9.00
Dwarfs, Bisque-like.......	10.00-12.00
2nd Row:	
Musicians (Two of Set of Six).........	6.00-7.00
Figures 2,3,4...........	8.00-9.00
3rd Row:	
Cherub Musicians, Bisque-like..........	10.00-12.00
4th Row:	
Baseball Bears (Pink, Blue, Green Colors)..........	6.00-6.50
Set: Pitcher, Batter, Catcher and Spectator	
Cherub Musician Bud Vases	7.00-8.00
5th Row:	
Elves, Sets of 6 or 8	
Planter Backs..........	15.00-17.50
Sans Planters..........	12.50-15.00

Page 98
Top Row:	
Ladies...............	7.50-8.50
2nd Row:	
Lady w/Parasol..........	8.00-9.00
Boy w/Bag............	9.00-10.00
Old Woman w/Balloons....	22.50-25.00
Bullfighter..............	8.00-9.00
Boy, Gold and White......	10.00-12.00
Bottom:	
Lady w/Basket..........	8.00-9.00
Colonial Man...........	5.00-6.00
Last Two Ladies........	6.00-7.00

Page 100
Top Row:	
All.................	6.00-7.00
2nd Row:	
1st and 5th Ladies.......	6.00-7.00
2nd Lady..............	5.00-6.00
3rd and 4th...........	7.00-8.00
6th Lady.............	6.00-7.00
3rd Row:	
All.................	5.00-6.00
4th Row:	
1st Lady Seated..........	4.00-5.00
2nd and 4th Seated Men...	6.00-7.00
3rd Man.............	4.50-5.00
5th Lady.............	4.00-5.00

Page 102
Top Row:	
1st, 4th, 6th...........	6.00-7.00
2nd and 5th Lady.......	10.00-12.00
3rd Seated Man........	12.50-15.00
Middle:	
1st Lady..............	6.00-7.00
2nd Seated Lady........	10.00-12.00
3rd Lady w/Dog........	10.00-12.00
Bottom:	
1st Gal.............	12.50-15.00
Men................	10.00-12.00
3rd and 5th Ladies.......	12.50-15.00

Page 104
Top Row:	
Small Turbaned Boy......	6.00-7.00
Large Turbaned Boy......	15.00-17.50
Hula Dancer...........	10.00-12.00
2nd Row:	
Canadian Policeman.......	9.00-10.00
Uncle Sam............	32.50-35.00
Large Cowboy..........	12.50-15.00
Small Cowboy..........	10.00-12.00
3rd Row:	
Matador.............	8.00-9.00
Cowgirl..............	12.50-15.00
Incense Burners.........	13.50-15.00
Cowgirl, Right..........	10.00-12.00
4th Row:	
Indian...............	12.00-14.00
Indian in Canoe.........	5.00-6.00
Cowgirl..............	12.50-15.00
Indian Incense Burner.....	15.00-17.50

Page 106
Clock................	125.00-150.00

PRICE GUIDE FOR OCCUPIED JAPAN II

Page 6
Top Row:
Chickens . . . . pr 17.50-20.00
Dog 8.00-10.00
Woebegone Horse 9.00-11.00
Second Row:
1st Dog, 7" 12.50-15.00
2nd & 3rd Dogs 10.00-12.50
Elephant 7.50-9.00
Bird 12.00-15.00
Third Row:
Frogs 12.00-15.00
Dog 7.00-8.00
Cat on Bed/Set 12.00-15.00
Lamb 6.00-7.00
Fourth Row:
Frog 10.00-12.00
Dog/Set (3) 7.50-10.00
Rabbit/Set (4)/Dated 17.50-20.00
Fifth Row:
Bees 6.00-7.50
Elephants on Wood/Set 15.00-17.50
Cat 4.00-5.00
Cat (Black Celluloid) 10.00-12.00
Scotties (Celluloid) 6.00-8.00
Page 8
Top Row:
Dogs 12.50-15.00
Bird 12.00-15.00
Frog (Bisque) 15.00-17.50
Second Row:
Birds 7.50-9.00
Dog 7.00-9.00
Geese (Blue Base, Set 3) 15.00-17.50
Goose Pruning Feathers 5.00-6.50
Third Row:
Bird 3.00-3.50
Dog (Rubber/Scottie) 7.50-9.00
Dog and Hydrant 9.00-12.50
Penguin 6.00-7.00
Dog with Ribbon 7.00-8.00
Fourth Row:
Dogs, (First Three) 4.00-6.00
Dog (Gray Dachshund) 12.00-15.00
Dog (Celluloid) 4.00-6.00
Fifth Row:
Bird 3.00-4.00
Swan 3.00-4.00
Monkey 3.50-5.00
Deer 5.00-6.00
Duck (Humanoid) 12.50-15.00
Page 10
Top Row:
Cigarette Box and Tray 17.50-20.00
Coal Scuttle and Tray 15.00-17.50
Second Row:
Pirate Snuffer 7.50-9.00
Man with Fly on Nose 15.00-17.50
Kentucky Map 12.00-15.00
Third Row:
Frog on Lily Pad 10.00-12.50
Elephants with Trays 17.50-20.00
"Wedgwood-Like" Tray 10.00-12.50
Fish 3.00-5.00
Bridge Set . . . . ea 3.00-3.50
Page 12
Top Row:
Sugar and Creamer on a
Tray 15.00-20.00
Cowboy Hat Ash Tray (5"
Width) 8.00-10.00

Candlestick, Pair 15.00-17.50
Tumbler (5 Oz.) 6.00-7.50
Second Row:
Desk Set (Exceptional Quali-
ty) 25.00-30.00
Match or Cigarette Holders . 5.00-6.00
Third Row:
Piano Jewelry Holder 15.00-17.50
Candy Container (Handled) . 12.00-15.00
Antimony Desk Set 25.00-30.00
Fourth Row:
Ash Tray 3.00-3.50
Ash Tray, Souvenir of
Alaska 5.00-6.00
Page 14
Top Row:
Dragon Mug (Engraved
"Sue") 12.00-15.00
Cigarette Holder 4.00-5.00
Tea or Spice Canister 10.00-12.00
Second Row:
Leaf Candy Dish 10.00-12.00
Salt & Pepper Shakers 8.00-10.00
Salt & Pepper Shakers on
Tray 10.00-12.00
Open Candy Dish 8.00-10.00
Piano Cigarette Dispenser . . 20.00-25.00
Third Row:
Jewelry Boxes, 5 Assorted
Sizes 10.00-15.00
Open Candy Dish 10.00-12.00
Hand Warmer & Chamois
Bag 25.00-30.00
Butter Dish 12.50-15.00
Sugar & Creamer, Pair 12.50-15.00
Fourth Row:
Cowboy Ash Tray 3.50-5.00
Heart Ash Tray
(Hot Springs, Ark.) 4.00-5.00
Cowboy Hat Ash Tray (3"
Wide) 5.00-6.00
Page 16
Top Row:
Red Haired Doll 30.00-35.00
Blue Dressed Doll 25.00-30.00
Japanese Set of Dolls in Box 50.00-55.00
Second Row:
Football Player Doll 12.00-15.00
Baseball Players 12.00-15.00
Doll in White Gown 35.00-40.00
Third Row:
Pink Teddy Bear 17.50-20.00
Doll in Blue (3" Composi-
tion) 25.00-30.00
Cat, Dog, Camel . . . . ea 9.00-10.00
Page 18
Top Row:
Mechanical Santa and
Reindeer 35.00-40.00
Football Pin 6.00-7.00
Rudolph, 7" 15.00-17.50
Small Reindeer 7.50-8.50
Second Row:
Rickshaw 12.00-15.00
Mechanical Santa 30.00-35.00
Third Row:
Stagecoaches 12.00-15.00
Goggles 6.00-7.50
Floating Water Lily 5.00-7.00
Mechanical Scottie with
Shoe 20.00-22.50

Christmas Bulbs in Box 17.50-20.00
Page 20
Tea Sets—Place Settings
Two 17.50-20.00
Three 25.00-30.00
Four 35.00-40.00
Four with Toureen and
Platter 45.00-50.00
Five 55.00-60.00
Six 65.00-75.00
Tray, Sugar, Creamer,
Teapot 22.00-25.00
Tray, Sugar and Creamer . . . 17.50-20.00
Bath Set, 3 Pieces 20.00-22.50
Page 22
Top Row:
1st and 5th Sets, Hexagonal 10.00-12.50
2nd Set 6.00-7.50
3rd and 4th Sets 7.00-8.50
Second Row:
1st Cup Only 8.00-9.00
2nd Set 10.00-12.50
3rd Set 12.50-15.00
4th (Satsuma) Set 17.50-20.00
5th Dragon Set 15.00-17.50
Third Row:
1st, 3rd, 4th Sets 10.00-12.50
2nd Set, Flower Petal 17.50-20.00
5th Set, Blue Willow 12.00-15.00
Fourth Row:
1st, 4th, 5th Sets 10.00-12.50
2nd, 3rd Sets 12.50-15.00
Page 24
Top Row:
Sweetmeat 90.00-100.00
Clock 45.00-50.00
Second Row:
Pastoral Scene Plate 65.00-75.00
Fall and Spring Plates . . . ea 12.50-15.00
Square Plate 10.00-12.50
Page 26
Top Row:
Gold Decorated Plate 15.00-17.50
Pagoda Plate 12.00-13.50
Second Row:
Scenic Plate 8.00-10.00
Octagonal Plate 10.00-12.50
Small Leaf Plate 3.50-4.50
Third Row:
Square Bowl 12.50-15.00
Plate with Ladies 17.50-20.00
Maple Leaf Plate 5.50-7.50
Japanese Scenic Plate 15.00-17.50
Flowered Bowl 8.00-10.00
Fourth Row:
Small Star Shaped Items . . . 4.00-5.50
Page 28
4 Place Setting w/Serving
Pieces 125.00-150.00
6 Place Setting w/Serving
Pieces 200.00-250.00
8 Place Setting w/Serving
Pieces 250.00-300.00
12 Place Setting w/Serving
Pieces 300.00-500.00
Page 34
"Blue Willow" Grill Plate . . 10.00-12.00
Salad Plate 6.00-8.00
Platter 20.00-25.00
"Old Willoware" Cup and
Saucer 12.00-15.00
"Gold Castle" Soup Bowl . . 6.00-8.00

Devil	25.00-30.00
Fourth Row:	
1st Toby	15.00-17.50
2nd Toby	17.50-20.00
Indian	25.00-30.00
Page 70	
Top Row:	
Stein Imitation	13.00-15.00
Bunny Handled Mug	17.50-20.00
Endowed Lady Handled	
Mug	20.00-25.00
Second Row:	
1st, 3rd People Handled	
Mugs.............ea	15.00-17.50
Bickering Mug (Possibly of	
Set)	18.00-20.00
Third Row:	
All Mugs	15.00-17.50
Fourth Row:	
Nude Lady Handled Mug	17.50-20.00
Parson Toby	50.00-65.00
Gentleman Toby	17.50-20.00
Page 72	
Top Row:	
Cowboy and Dutch Girl..ea	12.00-15.00
Japanese Girl	12.00-15.00
Vase (Richly Painted, Gold	
Trim)	12.50-15.00
Second Row:	
Vases	3.00-5.00
Dog and Birds	4.00-5.00
Man	5.00-6.00
Third Row:	
Rabbits and Blue Vases..ea	5.00-6.50
Scottie Dogs	5.00-7.50
Fourth Row:	
Ox Cart	4.50-6.00
Pig	8.00-9.00
Accordian Player	3.50-4.00
Spotted Dog	5.00-6.00
Scottie	4.50-6.00
Fifth Row:	
Vases	2.00-4.00
Animals	5.00-6.00
Page 74	
Top Row:	
Village (10 Pieces)	25.00-30.00
Football Player	7.50-9.00
Second Row:	
Cars In Original Boxes	20.00-25.00
Wooden Puzzle	8.00-10.00
Rubber Knife	7.50-9.00
Third Row:	
Football	15.00-17.50
Checkers	10.00-12.50
Razzers	5.00-6.00
Page 76	
Top Row:	
1st, 6th and 7th Vases...ea	10.00-12.00
2nd, "Wedgwood" Vase	4.00-5.00
3rd, 4th and 5th Vases	
(3½-4″)............ea	6.00-7.50
Second Row:	
1st and 6th Vase........ea	5.00-7.50
2nd, 3rd, 4th Vases.....ea	15.00-17.50
5th Vase	17.50-20.00
Third Row:	
1st and 5th, Pair	20.00-25.00
2nd, 3rd, 4th Vases.....ea	25.00-30.00
Fourth Row:	
1st Vase	17.50-20.00
2nd Vase	20.00-22.50
Dragon Vase	50.00-60.00
Page 78	
Top Row:	
Man, 15½″	65.00-75.00
Lady, 14½″	50.00-60.00

Second Row:	
Cupid and Swan	27.50-30.00
Cupid Artist	45.00-50.00
Cupid Standing	25.00-30.00
Third Row:	
"Hummel-like" boy and girl	
ea	20.00-25.00
Cupid and Heart	45.00-50.00
Seated Musician	20.00-25.00
Page 80	
Top Row:	
Bust of Man	22.50-25.00
Lady Vase	22.50-25.00
Second Row:	
Caped Boy and Girl......ea	20.00-22.50
Mexican with Donkey (Ap-	
prox. 8″)	20.00-22.50
Lady with Basket	17.50-20.00
Third Row:	
Colonial Man	12.00-15.00
Japanese Samurai	17.50-20.00
Peasant Girl Planter	30.00-35.00
Page 82	
Top Row:	
1st, 2nd, 4th and 5th	
Children	6.50-7.50
3rd Boy and Boy with Pig	10.00-12.50
Second Row:	
Girl on Fence	12.50-15.00
Girl in Cape	12.50-15.00
Girl with Geese	20.00-25.00
Girls with Baskets......ea	20.00-25.00
Third Row:	
Musicians	10.00-12.00
Fourth Row:	
Girl with Doll	8.00-10.00
Girl with Accordian	8.50-10.00
Baby with Bee	12.50-15.00
Double Figure with	
Umbrella	10.00-12.50
Tiny Girl in Green	3.50-4.50
Page 84	
Top Row:	
Boy and Girl (Approx. 8	
inches)............ea	20.00-25.00
...................pr	60.00
Second Row:	
Girl and Doll	30.00-35.00
Children with Boat	30.00-35.00
Children with Umbrella	30.00-35.00
Third Row:	
Walking Boy (Larger of	
Two)	20.00-25.00
Artist and Palette	30.00-35.00
Umbrella Boy	20.00-25.00
Walking Boy (Smaller of	
Two)	12.50-15.00
Hiker	12.50-15.00
Fourth Row:	
Girls with Geese	20.00-25.00
Girl Feeding Geese	15.00-17.50
Girls with Baskets.....ea	20.00-25.00
Page 86	
Top Row:	
Lady and Gentleman, Paired	
............ea	25.00-30.00
Second Row:	
Dutch Children........ea	15.00-20.00
Lady Holding Hat	17.50-20.00
Dancing Lady	17.50-20.00
Third Row:	
Tambourine Player	20.00-25.00
Dancer	25.00-30.00
Tiered Skirted Lady	25.00-30.00
Page 88	
Top Row:	
Green Pixies..........ea	12.50-15.00

Planter Pixie	15.00-17.50
Second Row:	
Elves Riding In-	
sects/Animals	22.50-25.00
Third Row:	
Mushroom Elves	10.00-12.00
Elf Astride Insect	22.50-25.00
Fourth Row:	
Pink Suited Elves	15.00-17.50
Page 90	
Top Row:	
First and Third Couple...ea	25.00-30.00
Coach	45.00-50.00
Second Row:	
Couple with Bench, Artist	
Signed	25.00-30.00
Standing Couple	27.50-30.00
Seated Couple	17.50-20.00
Seated Couple, Small,	
Artist Signed	20.00-25.00
Third Row:	
1st and 3rd Courting Couple	22.50-25.00
Seated Red Haired Couple	12.50-15.00
Bottom Row:	
Oriental Couple	20.00-22.50
Dutch Children Toothbrush	
Holder	20.00-25.00
Page 92	
Top Row:	
Girl, 12″ Tall	22.50-25.00
2nd and 5th Dancers	20.00-22.50
3rd and 4th..........ea	17.50-20.00
Second Row:	
1st and 6th Small Figures	8.50-10.00
2nd and 5th Men, Nice	
Detail..............ea	20.00-25.00
3rd Girl with Fan	10.00-12.50
4th Male Musician	10.00-12.00
Third Row:	
1st and 5th Small Figures	
...................ea	6.00-7.00
2nd Performer, Mate to	
Above	8.50-10.00
Reclining Man	10.00-12.50
Couple	8.50-10.00
Page 94	
Top Row:	
Oriental Pair	50.00-55.00
Trousered Oriental Pair	45.00-50.00
Second Row:	
First Pair Orientals	35.00-40.00
Black Based Orientals	30.00-35.00
Third Row:	
Coolie Hatted Pair	22.50-25.00
Animated Pair Orientals	25.00-30.00
Fourth Row:	
Flared Trousered Pair	30.00-35.00
Second Pair	30.00-35.00
Page 96	
Top Row:	
Colonial Couple........pr	100.00-125.00
Second Row:	
Couple in Blue and Pink, 12″	75.00-85.00
Third Row:	
Hatted Pair, Approx. 12″	60.00-75.00
Couring Couple, Approx. 12″	60.00-75.00
Bottom Row:	
Musicians Couple, Approx.	
10″	50.00-60.00
Seated pair, 6″	30.00-35.00
Page 98	
Top Row:	
Hatted Colonials, Approx.	
12″...............pr	50.00-60.00
Red Haired Colonials, 11½″	
...................pr	35.00-40.00

141

Books by Gene Florence

Collectors Encyclopedia of Depression Glass $19.95

Pocket Guide to Depression Glass $9.95

Collectors Encyclopedia of Occupied Japan I $12.95

Collectors Encyclopedia of Occupied Japan II $14.95

Collectors Encyclopedia of Occupied Japan III $19.95

Elegant Glassware of the Depression Era $19.95

Kitchen Glassware of the Depression Years $19.95

Add $1.00 postage for the first book, $.35 for each additional book.

Copies of these books may be ordered from:

Gene Florence
P.O. Box 22186
Lexington, KY 40522

or

COLLECTOR BOOKS
P.O. Box 3009
Paducah, KY 42001

Two Important Tools For The
Astute Antique Dealer, Collector and Investor

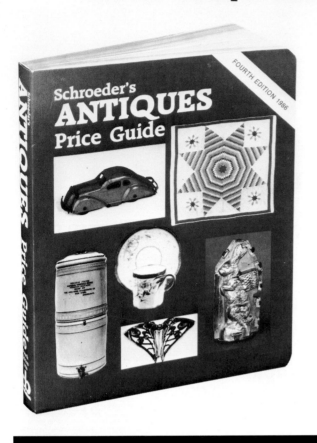